DAILY HOMILIES
Seasonal & Sanctoral

DAILY HOMILIES
Seasonal & Sanctoral
Advent, Christmas, Lent & Easter and all
Obligatory Memorials

by

Rev. S. Joseph Krempa

In Three Volumes

Volume 1 Ordinary Time—Year I
Volume 2 Ordinary Time—Year II
Volume 3 Seasonal & Sanctoral

ALBA · HOUSE NEW · YORK
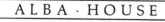
SOCIETY OF ST. PAUL, 2187 VICTORY BLVD., STATEN ISLAND, NEW YORK 10314

Library of Congress Cataloging in Publication Data

Krempa, S. Joseph.
  Daily homilies.

    Contents: v. 1. Ordinary Time—year I;
v. 2. Ordinary Time—year II;
v. 3. Seasonal and sanctoral, Advent, Christmas,
Lent & Easter, and all obligatory memorials.
    1. Catholic Church—Sermons. 2. Sermons, American.
3. Christian saints—Biography. I. Title.
BX1756.K782D34   1984   252'.6   84-24224
ISBN 0-8189-0480-1 (vol. I)
ISBN 0-8189-0481-X (vol. II)
ISBN 0-8189-0479-8 (vol. III)
ISBN 0-8189-0483-6 (set)

Nihil Obstat:
Rev. Thomas E. Crane

Imprimatur:
Most Rev. Edward D. Head
Bishop of Buffalo
November 13, 1984

Designed, printed and bound in the United States of
America by the Fathers and Brothers of the
Society of St. Paul, 2187 Victory Boulevard,
Staten Island, New York 10314, as part of their
communications apostolate.

3 4 5 6 7 8 9 (Current Printing: first digit).

PREFACE

During the week, a Mass celebrant encounters three groups of people: those who come daily, others who attend regularly and some who participate occasionally. A homilist has an obligation to each of these groups. One writer has compared it to preaching to a parade. Each day's scriptural selection is presented here with an exegetical and theological integrity of its own. Thematic unity for daily participants is balanced, however, by regular summaries so that the needs of the occasional participant are not disregarded.

The liturgical sense — the spiritual message as proclaimed — dominates these homilies although their deep background is based on technical analysis. A five minute reflection cannot be an occasion for a proper discussion of chiastic structure, Lukan sutures and the various levels of biblical criticism for people whose interests are more immediate and personal. Excellent and useful treatments of scriptural literary analysis abound, thankfully.

The section on obligatory memorials contains brief, preachable comments for memorials, most of which float without proper readings. These comments are not intended to supplant the detailed lives of the saints that are available.

At the conclusion of this lengthy work, some important acknowledgments are necessary. I would like to thank Archbishop Thomas Kelly of Louisville, Kentucky for his inspiration and example; Rev. Vincent Donovan of Laurel, Maryland for his discursive, but always insightful, Monday morning conversations; the Woodstock Theological Center Library at Georgetown University in Washington, D.C. for the generous permission to use their collection; special thanks to the community at the daily evening Mass at St. Nicholas Church in Laurel, Maryland whose patience, faith and encouragement made this book possible.

A distinct word of gratitude to my Ordinary, Bishop Edward Head of Buffalo, New York for his kindness. He is a man of extraordinary common sense who, over the past decade, has healed a diocese. Through his deep trust in everything Catholic, he has made Western New York a home for a wide, lively and diverse Catholic family.

Rev. S. Joseph Krempa

to Rev. Eugene Weber,
priest of West Virginia,
magnificent pastor,
sure guide on the Christian journey
who brings the Word to life every day

ADVENT and CHRISTMAS

MONDAY — First Week of Advent
Is 2:1-5,4:2-6   *Mt 8:5-11*

First Reading

Advent is a quietly reflective season of the Church year. It reminds us that we live in the space between the first coming of Jesus in Bethlehem and the second coming of Christ in majesty. In this spiritual and historical interim, we try to catch signs or previews of that coming era of the Messiah. The readings on these weekdays of Advent capture some insights into that future time for which we wait and pray. Today's first reading points to the unity of all people.

A   Isaiah draws a picture of all people invited into the glory of the Lord. It is his way of describing the purpose of creation. To the extent that we bring people together and seek reconciliation, we are fulfilling what the world was originally programmed to be. To the extent that we divide people and feed animosity, we introduce further dysfunction into creation.

B, C   Isaiah paints a powerfully vivid picture of this unity as we see people of every race and economic bracket streaming to the mountain of the Lord. Isaiah saw this focal point as the Jerusalem Temple. We know it as Jesus Christ. It will be a time of peace when the energies of aggression will be transferred into preserving peace. It is a vision of the end and purpose of our world.

Gospel Reading

This Gospel reading is more than a story of a soldier's faith. In this cameo appearance, the centurion represents the non-Jewish world. Deep within every human being is a capacity for faith, a love for peace and a desire for God. However we might suppress, hide and deface that instinct, it remains embedded within us as a quiet yearning for peace on earth. It is evidence of God's original plan that shows up with extraordinary power at Christmas.

Point

Advent reminds us that Isaiah's vision of unity is not one man's dream but a search that occupies all people. If we can manage to express some part of this unity, Christmas becomes more a faith experience than a holiday.

TUESDAY — First Week of Advent
Is 11:1-10   *Lk 10:21-24*

First Reading

Isaiah describes the Messiah as coming from the stump of Jesse (David's father). That great family tree of David had become over time a barren stump. Suddenly, there is a sprout, then a bud, now a blossom. This descendant of David, Isaiah tells us, will be filled with wisdom, understanding, fortitude... everything lacking in the kings after David. In a string of majestic images, he describes the Messiah's doing justice and restoring harmony throughout nature between lions and lambs, children and cobras.

This world of the Messiah is still in the process of being

born. Advent is a time to prepare for its birth: the birth of Christ to us with new power. Birthing is a painful process. The birth of Christ to us is not easy. We need others to assist us.

Gospel Reading

The seventy-two followers of Jesus were thrilled that they could expel demons in Jesus' name. At that, Jesus rejoices that His powers of life and restoration flowed to others through His disciples. It meant that the Church would work! Jesus "rejoiced in the Holy Spirit." Then, privately, He tells His disciples that this is how Isaiah's vision of restoration would come about: person to person. The slow birthing of the age of the Messiah.

Point

We are all midwives helping to bring forth Christ in one another.

WEDNESDAY — First Week of Advent
Is 25:6-10   *Mt 15:29-37*

First Reading

The Advent readings describe the Messianic era both as a moment toward which history is attracted and as a dimension of our present personal experience. Today's readings connect a chain of symbols spiralling in and out of the mystery of faith. In this first reading, Isaiah describes the "Messianic banquet" as a great celebration which God will provide for all of us after the veil of fear and suspicion is gone. People of every race and nationality will gather as brothers and sisters. This is a very graphic image of God's purpose and intent for creation. It is an image of what the Lord does in today's Gospel reading.

Gospel Reading

Jesus feeds the people in a traditional Gospel symbol of the Eucharist. We gather at this Eucharist to meet the Lord sacramentally and to be nourished by Him. This liturgy is a symbol of the final goal of our spiritual life: eternal communion with God together.

The power of these symbols depends on our experience. The effect of Isaiah's banquet metaphor relies on our memory of family dinners. The depth of our celebration is a function of what we bring to it and not simply of what we experience here. A person of deep spirituality is able to see in our liturgical action not only Isaiah's vision coming to life but a pointer toward the future of mankind. This Eucharist becomes a profoundly sacramental moment of meeting Christ.

At this season of the year, we can easily be transported by Christmas euphoria. If we prepare ourselves in Advent to let Jesus come forth from the tomb of our heart as Lord of our life then Christmas becomes an enriching sacramental experience and, for us, the era of the Messiah will have begun.

Point

The most abiding part of Christmas is the change that we allow to take place within ourselves.

THURSDAY — First Week of Advent
Is 26:1-6   *Mt 7:21, 24-27*

First Reading

Advent is the premier time of faith when we await the coming of the Lord Jesus into our life with fresh vigor. In this first reading, Isaiah calls upon the faithful people to trust in the Lord. He describes the Lord as a rock that strengthens our faith. The ground of our faith is not a particular religious fashion or cultural fad. The moods of our time change rapidly. Isaiah tells us that a solid faith draws its strength from that on which it rests. If we are personally linked to the Lord, then our faith is as secure and power-filled as His Resurrection.

Gospel Reading

Anyone who hears the Lord's words and puts them into action is building on rock. We strengthen our faith by practicing it. Theory or emotion is fugitive. When we start to live out our faith, it slowly becomes a deeper and more insistent part of us. What is true of any field of study is true of our spiritual life. Practice roots and anchors theory. Spiritual maturity is not conceptual but practical. In Advent, we prepare not only for Christmas day but for something more lasting. We try to capture the Christmas spirit to make it our own. This has less to do with the atmospherics of the season than with the fellowship we share. If we ground our Christmas celebration on our experience of the Lord Jesus, then it will have effects that pour into every phase of our life.

Point

Christmas is more than a seasonal ambience. It is a way of life. Putting the significance of Christmas into regular practice is like building on rock — it lasts!

FRIDAY — First Week of Advent
Is 29:17-24   Mt 9:27-31

First Reading

In this first reading, Isaiah speaks of the deaf coming to hear, the blind beginning to see and the poor being invited to celebrate. This is more than a poetic ideal. A day when illness will be gone and the terror of natural disasters eliminated is not simply an object of wishful thinking. If all people lived under the Lordship of Christ, such things would begin to happen. If our resources were allocated to research and to the conquering of diseases, then one day the blind would see and the lame would walk. We can see the phenomenal progress made in the areas of heart disease, cancer, tuberculosis, polio and leprosy. If we established correct priorities, we would be able to learn to deal with natural disasters; societal arrangements would be more equitable. We would not throw food away in one part of our planet while millions starve a few thousand miles away.

Gospel Reading

The reign of the Messiah occurs on three levels. There is the universal level — the object of Israel's hope and of Christian prayer. It is a moment as inevitable as it is hidden in the Father's decision for the Lord's return. The second level is the local level of communities and families. This is the sphere of human kindness where we can see occasional sparking flashes of kingdom power. The third level is within ourselves. This is the level of grace where we experience peace and reconciliation. We can take stock of our distance from the kingdom. The Messiah's birth and the sending of the Pentecost Spirit imply that the kingdom of God can be experienced here on earth. We pray for, look for and work for the kingdom.

Point

The promise of Christmas is not only peace within ourselves but also peace on earth. It is the same gift in two sizes.

SATURDAY — First Week of Advent
Is 30:19-21, 23-26 *Mt 9:35-10:1, 6-8*

First Reading

After describing the coming judgment against Judah, Isaiah speaks of redemption and restoration. As he speaks these very words, the approaching exile of the Jewish people was only a distant rumble. But here, he looks through the pain to announce a time of no further weeping, no more want or groping for the truth. One day, he promises, we will see the Teacher and hear the voice that points out the direction in which we should travel. Isaiah speaks not of reward but of transformation. The coming pain of the exile would cleanse the blockages and allow people to again hear the word of the Lord. This experience would qualify them for the larger mission of bringing the wisdom gained out of this experience to the Gentiles.

Gospel Reading

We have Isaiah's "Teacher" — the Lord Jesus — sending His disciples first to the lost sheep of Israel. The Jewish people were the initial focus of Jesus' ministry. This was not only to fulfill prophecy. Israel's turbulent and painful past, its experience of the transience of glory and the agony of judgment should have prepared it more than any one else to receive the Gospel. Its experience of God, purified by the rhythm of defeat and victory, sin and redemption, was precisely its gift to the world. The potential harvest among such a people was very great.

Point

Our spiritual struggles are not ours alone. Insight is a gift and a responsibility. Christmas is a time to share not only material gifts but the spiritual wisdom distilled from our life experience.

MONDAY — Second Week of Advent
Is 35:1-10   *Lk 5:17-26*

First Reading

In this vision of the Messianic age, Isaiah sees the planet transformed into a paradise of natural beauty and human wholeness. A single word that sums up this majestic vision is restoration. Jesus came to restore people and societal structures to the health and harmony intended by God from the very beginning. He came to break apart the power of evil, to give new vitality to our relationships with others, and to bring new light to our inner selves. This spiritual revival which the Lord brings will eventuate into a concrete restoration of our world. The fulfillment of Isaiah's towering vision is delayed in its coming by our sin. The new world he beholds has begun in Christ. Its completion depends upon us.

Gospel Reading

In today's Gospel reading, we see the in-breaking of the power of the Messianic era. In Jesus' forgiveness of sin and restoration of human health, a world is being born again. One great gift of Christmas for which Advent prepares us is the glimpse we have for a few hours of that restored world where the broken can be made whole. For those few short hours, the Word leaps down from heaven and lives and laughs among us.

Point

The restoration Jesus brings is not simply spiritual. It is total.

TUESDAY — Second Week of Advent
Is 40:1-11   *Mt 18:12-14*

First Reading

This first reading is from a second prophet called Isaiah of Babylon who wrote at the end of Judah's exile. He is the spokesman for the new mission of Judah in a new era. In this reading, he describes a magnificent parade, actually more of an exodus, out of Babylon through the desert toward the new Jerusalem. God is repeating in a new way what was once done through Moses. We can take the time to examine our own personal place of exile, the place or condition of distress that we wish to leave, the area of our life where we feel displaced. Christmas is the promise of our exodus, a period of discipline and transition. It is not a journey that we make alone, however. The Lord is with us as He was with the Israelites in their travels to their promised land.

Gospel Reading

Jesus particularizes Isaiah's vision for us. The great exodus takes shape in the life, death and Resurrection of the Lord Jesus. Not only does the Lord's Spirit guide history and the Church but our individual lives as well. The Lord actively seeks us out, like a shepherd, to provide a way home. We should not forget that in our own lives, we live out the great events of salvation history. We experience call, exile, exodus, promise, covenant, passion, death and resurrection. The great cycle of salvation repeats itself in every life.

Point

We are not travelling blind. The Lord guides us if we are willing to follow Him.

WEDNESDAY — Second Week of Advent
Is 40:25-31   *Mt 11:28-30*

First Reading

This second prophet called Isaiah makes a unique conjunction in this reading between the new exodus which the Lord promises and a new creation. He describes a Creator God who did not simply create and step back to watch things happen. God continues to create through the renewal of vigor and strength that societies, communities and individuals experience. Each moment of new courage, renewed faith, new birth, reconciliation and reborn love is a fresh creative act of God. By his linking of the seminal Creation and Exodus traditions, Isaiah reminds us that the creative activity of God is not a past event but is active in our lives. God is able to do something new for us. At Christmas, when families and friends renew their links of love, we experience a new surge of God's creative, life-giving power.

Gospel Reading

Succinctly and warmly, the Lord describes the revival and refreshment He gives to the weary. In the middle of all the hectic activity of the season, it is important that we take time to stop, lay down our burdens and concentrate on the Lord's love for us shown through the circumstances of His birth in Bethlehem. The Church year provides many ways of viewing His love. We can do so through His sufferings, His ministry, His Resurrection, His gift of the Spirit. But Christmas is the time to look at the baby in Bethlehem to capture a fresh vision of God's love for us. It can provide a new angle from which to view our faith and discipleship.

Point

Revival and re-creation are as much demonstrations of God's power as the very first sparks of Genesis.

THURSDAY — Second Week of Advent
Is 41:13-20   *Mt 11:11-15*

First Reading

Let us try to recapture the bite of the word "redeemer" which Isaiah of Babylon uses.It is a word used so often that we are forgetful of its original context. It was a legal term as much for the Jews as it is for us. It refers to the process of buying something back. The Book of Leviticus states: "When your brother sells himself to a stranger, he shall have the right of redemption after he has sold himself. Any blood relative may redeem him." The one who bought back such a slave was a "redeemer." Isaiah states that since God made the Jews His own people, He is bound to them by covenant blood. Now, He will "redeem" them from exile. We sell ourselves to every sort of power and ambition. Jesus, our blood brother, buys us back. It is not blasphemous to keep the commercial background of the word in our minds. It provides a helpful point of view on an ancient mystery of faith.

Gospel Reading

The Lord refers to John the Baptist, the classic Advent figure, who highlighted the importance of preparation. A slave's chains can be broken while he does not realize it. The purpose of Advent is to remind us that our Redeemer has come. We are free to leave the prison. So often, people do not fully apprehend the freedom they have in the Lord and continue to live as slaves. The Baptist and Advent serve to remind us that we have been redeemed. We are free from the power and chains of sin. We have only to accept the freedom.

Point

The real freedom from the power of sin we have been given by Christ must be accepted by us for it to be psychologically and emotionally effective.

FRIDAY — Second Week of Advent
Is 48:17-19   *Mt 11:16-19*

First Reading

The Redeemer speaks through Isaiah to remind us to keep His commandments. We can look at the Commandments through the wrong end of the telescope to see them as prohibitions — a catalogue of forbidden behaviors: stealing, murder, adultery. The word of the Lord in this first reading speaks of something much broader than that. The Redeemer God speaks to us of an entire way of life. The phrase "commandments" implies an entire ensemble of attitudes, assumptions and ways of dealing with people and property that cannot be exhaustively itemized. It refers to a mindset, a way of living that is life-giving rather than death-dealing.

Gospel Reading

Although Advent is not a penitential season, it is a time of serious preparation. Personal change is very difficult to effect. We all gather various pretexts for avoiding it. The Lord describes two of them in today's Gospel reading. People refuse the call to change because the caller is either too conservative and ascetic or too liberal and insufficiently penitential. Jesus compares these critics to children who want to play a different game from the one suggested. We can all find hundreds of pretexts to avoid the difficult work of change. The same can happen to our Advent. We can find many diversions during the holiday season to delay the soul-searching and spiritual preparation that gives real liturgical and spiritual energy to Advent.

Point

A cosmetic Advent leads to a cosmetic Christmas.

SATURDAY — Second Week of Advent
Si 48:1-4, 9-11   *Mt 17:10-13*

First Reading

A legend surrounded the fiery figure of Elijah. He appeared suddenly during a time of pagan hysteria in the north. He challenged the pagan practices of Jezebel, threw down the gauntlet to her pagan prophets, stood firmly on the ancient covenant faith and was finally taken from the earth in a chariot of fire. This gave birth to the belief that he did not die but wandered the earth only to return one day to set things right before the coming of the Messiah. That is Sirach's reference in today's first reading. One day, in the Judean wilderness, the

Baptist appeared dressed as Elijah. For those who knew the prophecies, this was an event of great significance.

Gospel Reading

In this post-Transfiguration scene, Jesus reminds His disciples that Elijah had indeed come in the person of John the Baptist. It was one more piece of corroborating evidence of Jesus' Messiahship. Peter had admitted Jesus to be the Messiah. Jesus then told the disciples that both Messiah and disciples would have to suffer. This disconcerted them so deeply that they needed the Transfiguration experience to strengthen their faith. After seeing Moses and Elijah in conversation with the Lord, they realized that the momentous and awaited event of great redeeming significance was about to take place.

For the Lord to come to us in power as Messiah, we need to prepare ourselves. That is the function of our remembrance of the Baptist. He represents the self-examination that is the critical prelude to a deeply satisfying and redeeming Christmas experience.

Point

Through the liturgy, the Baptist still calls us to prepare a way in our hearts and lives for the coming of the Lord.

MONDAY — Third Week of Advent
Nb 24:2-7, 15-17   *Mt 21:23-27*

First Reading

Advent is a time when we collect many of the Old Testament incidents and prophecies that the early Church saw as pointing toward Christ. Today's first reading is a humorous episode during the time of Israel's gradual immigration into the promised land. The Moabites (whose country bordered on Palestine) were more than a little disconcerted by Israel's entry into and proprietary attitude toward their neighboring land. The king, Balak, had hired a free-lance prophet to curse Israel. Instead, the roving prophet-for-hire, Balaam, could only pronounce a blessing. In the course of his several oracles, this last has been taken as referring to the coming Messiah. He extolls the glory of Israel's presence in the land — not exactly what the Moabite king had paid him to say. He then predicts that a star shall proceed from the tribe of Jacob and a staff of leadership shall arise which signals the demise of the Moabites and the ascendancy of David and ultimately of Christ, both from the tribe of Jacob. Popular interpretation has seen the mention of the star as not metaphorical of leadership but as a real prediction of the guiding star of Matthew's infancy account. The larger meaning of the incident is the assurance that God will be faithful to His promise to Israel that they shall inherit the land despite Moabite opposition.

Gospel Reading

The opposition to the Lord is not Moabite but religious. It is one of many scenes where the religious leaders were testing and probing Jesus. Perhaps because the Lord saw they were manipulative in their questioning, He posed a counterquestion to force them to take a public stand in regard to the popular, martyred Baptizer. This they refused to do.

We come to a point in our life where we must decide how we shall live. During Advent, this issue focuses around the meaning the Incarnation has for us. Does the fact that God became a human being have any real-world consequences for my life and spirituality? Such a decision is important. It avoids our treating religion as a set of figurines that we can pull out of a box once or twice a year and then dismiss after the season is over.

Point

God did not become a human being so that we could have a holiday season. He came to transform lives and bring new fire into people's hearts.

TUESDAY — Third Week of Advent
Zp 3:1-2, 9-13   *Mt 21:28-32*

First Reading

Zephaniah is the prophet of the Day of wrath and mourning. He spoke God's word of judgment against Judah and its capital Jerusalem. In this first reading, he describes the purification God will effect against the pride and superficiality of Judah's religious practices. Very much a spiritual disciple of Isaiah, Zephaniah predicts a time when a remnant, embedded in Israel's life, full of humility and love of God, will survive to be the nucleus of a renewed Israel. It will energize all the nations into worship of the one, true God. It was from this core of humble, God-awaiting people that the Lord Jesus came. He embodied everything that Israel and Judah were called to be, but failed to become. Jesus was that obedient, humble servant who would be the epicenter of a new covenant.

Gospel Reading

This parable captures the difference between the superficial religion condemned by Zephaniah and the inner faith of that mysterious remnant which he saw as the key to universal salvation. Both sons were told to work in the Father's world. One gave great display of his obedience and, in fact, did nothing. His response was pious, deferential and insincere. The second son hesitated, but once in the world, he proceeded to do everything the Father requested. The contrast between the sons captures the difference between the outward expression of religious fervor without any practical application and the effort of those holy people of all ages who follow the light as best they can. In the final analysis, the depth of our celebration of the Incarnation will be measured not by the songs we sing and the sentiments we express but by the extent to which we extend ourselves to heal some wounds, help the hurting and bring support to those who have little else on which to rely.

Point

The test of obedience and faith is action. Zephaniah's remnant combines the two.

WEDNESDAY — Third Week of Advent
Is 45:6-8, 18, 21-25   *Lk 7:18-23*

First Reading

This prophecy of salvation, from the time of the exile, is steeped in strange, cryptic statements. "I am the Lord; I form the light and the darkness" — the Lord God is omnipotent and all things are of His making. What we call well-being and woe are the result of His creative hand. "Let justice descend. . .and spring out of the earth." The emergence of justice and holiness in our world is neither total gift nor complete human achievement. With the enabling power of God, justice can emerge from this mix of well-being and woe. The world is not finished. God created it to be a home and not a waste. He is present among us even now transforming creation from within. The great creative energy of God has now been bestowed on people in the form of the Holy Spirit through the death and Resurrection of Christ. The birth of Jesus was not an afterthought. The plan of salvation from the very beginning was that mankind have some share in the life and light of God. This ancient prophecy gives us a glimpse in Old Testament terms of the final triumph of Christ.

Gospel Reading

In Jesus' response to the messengers of the Baptist, we have a catalogue of the ways the Lord continues the work of creation and re-creation as He heals and restores sight, wholeness and life to people of the earth. In all the cures, moments of forgiveness and sessions of teaching, we see the Lord shaping, forming and creating a people of His own. Today, this work begun by the Lord in His earthly ministry continues through us His people. We are called to heal, assist the lame and enable those blinded to so many things to see more clearly. Christmas is our annual reminder that the great prophetic words of Isaiah, Zephaniah and the Advent prophets can become flesh in us. They need not remain cryptic words. We can give them texture, shape and power.

Point

The ancient prophecies continue to be fulfilled by Jesus through us.

THURSDAY — Third Week of Advent
Is 54:1-10   *Lk 7:24-30*

First Reading

The theme from this second (or possibly third) prophet called Isaiah is the fruitfulness of faith. The Lord speaks to an Israel that had become a barren, political non-entity. The Jewish people are told to make space in their tent, the Lord is moving in among them with a love that will never die. This prophecy carries many levels in itself. To the Jewish people whose kingly line had virtually become extinct — the family tree of Jesse became a stump — a savior is about to be born and a new family tree will come to life. We can apply these words to the Church, a minor political entity on the world stage, but awesome in the spiritual and moral power it commands. In our own lives, this prophecy assures us that however fragile our faith seems to be, the Lord is always ready to revive us and to release His spiritual power within us.

Gospel Reading

The great prophet, John the Baptist, is outranked by the smallest member of the kingdom. We cannot give this kingdom political shape or geographical boundaries because its dimensions, power and effects are primarily spiritual. Even though we cannot easily chart them, its effects can be seen in changed lives. We can see the movement of the Holy Spirit in persons, parishes and larger communities. Just as the kingdom of God is not measurable in financial or commercial terms, so our celebration of Christmas cannot be calibrated in financial or commercial terms. The real depth and enduring quality of our reflection on the Incarnation is whether it has an effect on how we live and love.

Point

*The power of the kingdom is found in its ability to em-
power others.*

FRIDAY — Third Week of Advent
Is 56:1-3, 6-8   Jn 5:33-36

First Reading

These words of Isaiah speak to a central thrust of the
Incarnation — its universal expansivity. If the Word of God
became flesh, it was to touch all flesh and blood. The power of
the Incarnation cannot be limited by geography, nationality or
religious affiliation. In some way, all people are changed because of the Incarnation. Because of Bethlehem, all people can
now receive the Holy Spirit in a way that was metaphysically
impossible before the Incarnation. The drive of the Incarnation
is to include all people within the ambit and circle of God's life
and love. Isaiah phrases this as calling all foreigners to the holy
mountain. When we apply this to ourselves, reference to the
universal reach of the Incarnation may seem too awesome for
us to comprehend in a practical way. However, in our own
neighborhoods and parishes are people, generally neglected
by others, who have been included in God's loving plan and
are waiting to be touched by Christ's hand. These are
minorities, the elderly and shut-ins who form the generally
invisible sectors of society who are waiting to experience for
themselves the good news which they hear preached so often.

Gospel Reading

Jesus speaks to the Jews of the various witnesses who can
testify to His identity. The Baptist was one witness. The more

convincing witness is the pattern of His ministry. If the Jews could not see the hand of God at work in the kind of life Jesus lived, they would be unable to see God anywhere. The same principle is true today. The rhetoric of faith is widely disseminated through the media and liturgy. The most convincing sign of the authenticity of our words is the work we do as Christians. It is our ability to translate the songs and scriptures of faith into concrete deeds of faith and love that provide the most convincing evidence of their truth. This kind of evidence is the most powerful sign we can give to a cynical age that we are the followers of Jesus and that He is of God.

Point

Christmas is a time for us to turn our faith and love into flesh and blood.

DECEMBER 17
Gn 49:2, 8-10   Mt 1:1-17

First Reading

As the Book of Genesis ends, Jacob gives a blessing to each of his twelve sons. These blessings are really retrospective forecasts of the fortunes of each of the tribes in later history. The blessing given to Judah has a double significance. It points, first of all, to the power of the lion and the royal dynasty that would emerge from the tribe of Judah. On this historical plane, the prophecy was fulfilled in King David of the tribe of Judah who was promised an everlasting dynasty from which the scepter would never depart. David was only an anticipatory sign of the greater Ruler Who would emerge centuries later in the person of Jesus of Nazareth, also of the tribe of Judah. His kingdom will last forever. Jacob's blessing, which had meandered its way through centuries of disappointment, found secure fulfillment in Jesus.

Gospel Reading

This is a famous Gospel reading that nobody likes to read. It seems to be only a series of names begetting other names. Just as any genealogy reveals a great deal about an individual, so Jesus' genealogy tells us a great deal about Him. These names evoke a rich and sacred drama. As they tumble out, we see Israel's movement from a loose web of tribes into an empire and then to an occupied state. It is a story of the spiritual maturation of a people from the days of Abraham's sacrifice to the Judaism of Jesus' day. Just as our family history is poured into us, so this entire Jewish panorama was poured into Jesus. He was every inch a Jew, in the full rush of Jewish history and tradition. He transformed the entire Jewish heritage that flowed through Him. He released the promise from its special attachment to a particular people and made it available to everyone. The majesty and failures of Judaism now belong to all of us. The great figures of the Old Testament are our spiritual ancestors in Christ.

Point

We are now the bearers of the new covenant.

DECEMBER 18
Jr 23:5-8   Mt 1:18-24

First Reading

The righteous shoot which Jeremiah describes would be a welcome relief to the Jewish people. After decades of corrupt and petty kings, he predicts the rise of a just and holy King who would lead the people to a new greatness. So pivotal would His reign be that no longer would His people be defined by the great Exodus event, but by His reign and the restoration He would bring. This is exactly what happened in Jesus. The new people created in His blood no longer define themselves exclusively by the great Exodus deliverance but by the new Passover of the death and Resurrection of Jesus. That passing-over became the core event around which the Lord's community built itself and which gave meaning to its future history. The final deliverance from sin has been accomplished. We now seek to integrate that deliverance into our lives and concretize it in our social and ecclesiastical structures.

Gospel Reading

As the early Church reflected and prayed over the great deliverance from sin achieved by Jesus' death and Resurrection, they gradually came to see that the decisive moment did not begin on Calvary. The kingdom had begun much earlier when the Word of God first became flesh at the moment of Jesus' conception. Matthew traces the beginning of the Day of salvation back to the Annunciation when Mary first consented to be an instrument of God's plan. In our own lives, the great breakthroughs in the realm of the spirit and in our personal ventures did not come from nothing. They were the end product of a great deal of effort and preparation. If we have known moments of deep personal peace, it is because we have battled for it and had long before decided to submit ourselves to the presence of the Holy Spirit. In the same way, the great Passover of the Lord on Holy Thursday, Good Friday and Easter Sunday did not come from nowhere. It was the end result of a lifetime of Jesus' obedience to the Father that began when Mary as a young woman said, "Let it happen as you say."

Point

Our simple moments of submission can give birth to periods of great achievement.

DECEMBER 19
Jg 13:2-7, 24-25   Lk 1:5-25

First Reading

This first reading recalls Samson, a great warlord or judge of Israel's history. He had sought revenge against the ever-unpopular Philistines and won. He was a national hero. Because of his success, the people traced back his beginnings to show that he was chosen by God from the start. In this first reading, Samson's mother dedicates him to God by making the Nazirite vow which included leaving one's hair uncut. It was a sign of loyalty to the traditional customs of the Hebrews. Enter Delilah. She cut his hair; he broke the vow; the rest is history. Samson's fate was as awful as the motion picture.

Gospel Reading

We have the same dedicatory theme in today's Gospel reading. There was a glut of priests in those days, so Zechariah had to wait his turn to offer sacrifice. John the Baptist had been so popular a figure that the people traced his beginnings back to show that he was chosen by God from the very start. We read about Samson and John on the verge of Christmas for two reasons. In trying to understand who Jesus was and what He did, the first Christians looked to familiar role models from their Jewish past. We do the same when we compare the style of a new president with those of his predecessors. It enables us to connect the new and unknown with the old and familiar. The models to which the early Christians looked were Moses, David, Samson the deliverer, John the Baptist. The remembered qualities of these heroes were all collected in Jesus. Secondly, Samson and John were chosen from their conception as was Jesus. Their role in salvation history was no accident. In the same way, the Incarnation was part of God's saving design. All the events of sacred history lead up to it, and the rest of salvation's story follows from it.

Point

Jesus, Samson and John were set apart by God for a special mission. The same is true of us.

DECEMBER 20
Is 7:10-14

Lk 1:26-38

First Reading

King Ahaz was caught between two sharks in this historical vignette. Whichever country he allied himself with would turn him into a puppet. Isaiah advises him to join no alliances but to rely on God's promises to David. Ahaz responds somewhat cynically and patronizingly that he will not tempt God. Isaiah then tells him of the sign he will receive — the birth of a baby whose seventh birthday will see the collapse of these unholy alliances. Christian tradition has looked to these words of Isaiah to see a prophecy of the coming Messiah in the Lord Jesus who would collapse all unholy alliances. Just as the birth of a son to Ahaz meant that David's family line would continue, so the birth of Jesus meant that this Davidic ruler would conquer our spiritual enemies and rule in glory. This Messiah would not only be the sign but the very fulfillment of God's promises to the people of Israel through David.

Gospel Reading

The fulfillment of Isaiah's prophetic message is seen in today's Gospel reading. The familiar annunciation scene is filled with the atmosphere, music, phrases and spiritual scenery of the Old Testament prophets.

Christmas is a time of strong emotion for everyone. During this season, we look to the past and to the future. In between, we try to arrange and experience some Christmas joy. This is exactly how the Church celebrates Christmas. We look back to our prophetic tradition to see its real meaning in the light of the Incarnation. We view the future in the light of the Incarnation and in between we try to prepare ourselves to experience Christmas joy. As time passes, we come to see the heart of Christmas not in the holiday atmosphere as much as in the hope, faith and joy that Christmas uncovers deep inside ourselves.

Point

Prayer and love are the heart of the Gospel and the heart of Christmas.

DECEMBER 21
Sg 2:8-14/Zp 3:14-18   *Lk 1:39-45*

First Reading

The Song of Songs has been traditionally interpreted to describe God's pursuit of humanity. Perhaps because the language is so earthy and physical, we have the unusual arrangement of an alternative first reading today. The strongly physical tone of the Song of Solomon might be too vivid for those who take an excessively spiritualistic view of religion. There is a tendency not to take the Incarnation seriously. The earliest heresies in the Church denied not the divinity but the humanity of Jesus. Even in our day, there is a view that sees the humanity of Jesus as so swamped by His divinity as to be seriously diminished. Such a reluctance to take the drive of the Incarnation seriously reflects itself in our view of the action and place of God in our lives. Some see human love and intelligence as too tainted to be instruments of God's saving work in our world. So, they await supernatural visions and spiritual spectaculars. Yet, the message of Bethlehem is that God has associated Himself with humanity for good as His best and brightest sacrament.

Gospel Reading

The reasons why Luke included the Visitation scene are significant. Not only did he want to show the close link between Jesus and John but also the inherent superiority of the Lord even at this early point in their existence. At its most obvious level, the Visitation is a sharing of joy and faith, something to which we Catholics are not accustomed. At Christmastime, we gather for the Christmas Mass but seldom talk with each other about the implications of the Incarnation. Each of us has a private theology of it which, regrettably, we keep private. We share food, time, presents with others. But the deepest, most personal and most memorable gift we have to share with others is our faith.

Point

Our relationship with the Lord is a spiritual extension of the Incarnation. To include others within it is a great gift at Christmas.

DECEMBER 22
1 S 1:24-28   *Lk 1:46-56*

First Reading

Samuel was a great figure in Israel's history. He guided their transition from a tribal league to a monarchy. This reading shows the origin of his power and influence in his dedication to God by his mother Hannah from the day of his birth. She vowed to the Lord that if a son were born to her, no razor would touch his head — that is, he would not follow Canaanite customs. He would be an Israelite right through the marrow of his bones. Hannah's canticle of thanksgiving following the long-awaited birth of her son is found in the responsorial psalm for today. It is a model for Mary's great hymn of thanksgiving. The faith of both mothers was not simply coincidental to their sons' greatness. A great deal of their faith passed into their sons.

Gospel Reading

The Magnificat celebrates the great reversals of history. The barren give birth; virgins conceive; those without faith are converted into great saints; the powerful trip up. If we look back over the past half century, we can review the great names that dominated the world scene a mere half century ago: Hitler, Mussolini, Haile Selassie, Franklin Roosevelt, Stalin. The philosophies, trends and fashions of those days are largely gone. God's justice rushes like a powerful current throughout the human story. It has washed to the side those who opposed it. Just as the spark of life deep within Mary was proof that the ancient promise would come true, so the spark of the Holy Spirit deep within us is proof that the Gospel promises will come true for each of us.

Point

Woven into the events of history and our lives is the mighty current of God's justice and grace.

DECEMBER 23
Ml 3:1-4, 23-24   *Lk 1:57-66*

First Reading

The prophet Malachi describes events that will precede the coming of the Messiah. The messenger and herald of the new covenant was rumored to be fiery old Elijah. Legend had it that he did not die but would return to set things right before the coming of the Lord. Elijah was totally dedicated to the God of Israel to the exclusion of the pagan gods that infested Israel during his lifetime. John the Baptist was a second Elijah. He was totally dedicated to the God of Israel and spoke words of judgment and repentance. He came forward dressed like Elijah with a message that made contemporary many of Elijah's demands centuries earlier. He was the great messenger of the Messiah.

Gospel Reading

John is given a name. We usually give the Baptist short shrift during the rest of the year. Matthew and Luke present rather elaborate stories about him. There were followers of John around even after the Lord's Resurrection. Paul encountered one of them in his missionary work. The Baptist was a complex figure and many thought that he might be the Messiah. It is for this reason that the Gospels go out of their way to show that he was simply the messenger to which Malachi referred. In the Gospels, John himself states that he is not the light; Jesus must increase; he is not worthy to loosen His sandalstrap. John's function was to point to Christ. Today, at the very edge of Christmas, we remind ourselves that the function of priests, parishes and liturgical ministers is to point to Christ; not to celebrate ourselves, our homiletic or musical virtuosity, but to celebrate the Lord. We are called at Christmas to do all in our power to bring home to people the love and depth of God's new relationship with humanity that began on that first Christmas night.

Point

He must increase, we must decrease.

DECEMBER 24
2 S 7:1-5, 8-11, 16   Lk 1:67-79

First Reading

David had wanted to build a temple to the Lord. God speaks through Nathan to tell him that past is prologue enough. Just as God had lived among His people in the desert and raised them from Egypt into a great nation, raising David in a similar fashion to a great monarch, so He would do the same in the future. It was not the presence or absence of a temple that would determine the greatness and power of God among the people. It would be His work among and with them that would show Him to be God. The great sign of God's presence is not granite or limestone but a spiritual dynasty to be born of David's line. In this royal dominion of a future ruler, God's love and presence would be made real, effective and abiding. God would dwell among people.

Gospel Reading

The Benedictus of Zechariah, the Baptist's father, is filled with Old Testament allusions to the glory of God and His promises to His people. It is the promise that God will be with His people in their darkest night. The hymn celebrates the prophet of the Most High, John the Baptist, who will prepare the way and the people. On this Christmas eve, we prepare in an immediate way for the celebration of the Lord's birth among us. The great promises to David have been fulfilled in the person of Mary and the family tree of Joseph. Mary was the true ark of the old and new covenants. In the dark deep of her body, one Testament came to an end as another began.

Christmas is a time for us to renew our covenant with the Lord. We look at the love and power of God that took shape in Mary's womb and came among us in a flush of blood and water both in Bethlehem and on the cross. From that very human event divine life forever became a human possibility. We now can be the Temples that house the glory of God.

Point

The long night of waiting is over. Now, we celebrate new birth in Bethlehem and in our lives.

DECEMBER 26
Ac 6:8-10;7:54-59   Mt 10:17-22

First Reading

Stephen was a much more complex figure than he is popularly pictured to be. The Book of Acts presents initially an idyllic picture of the life of the Christian community. Suddenly, the Greek Christians complain about the neglect of Greek widows among them. It seems there were two groups of Jewish Christians. There was a Palestinian group who spoke Aramaic and a non-Palestinian group who spoke Greek. To accommodate this latter group, the Twelve ordained deacons to serve the widows. Then, of a sudden, Stephen is doing a great deal more than waiting on widows. He is preaching like an Apostle and criticizing Temple and Torah as well. In a popular form of lynch law, the Jews stone him on the spot. The Book of Acts tells us that even this was part of God's design.

Gospel Reading

In the first reading, we see the fulfillment of what the Lord had said about persecution. We speak of martyrs, death and dissension so quickly after Christmas. We are reminded that the holiday is an idealized parenthesis in our life. After the season's greetings are over, politics, violence and threats return to the front pages of our newspapers. This is the real milieu of the Incarnation. The pivotal issue is not whether light shined in Bethlehem but whether light shines now, whether we can see light in darkness and our world in its true light. Early on, the Church discovered that discipleship was not a romantic interlude in a hostile world. With Christmas Day behind us, we are forced to focus on the Light without the melodic backdrop. The Light reveals things in the world we may never have seen before and things about ourselves we may never have realized.

Point

As we assimilate the meaning of the Incarnation, then the Light shines out from within us into the darkness.

DECEMBER 27
1 Jn 1:1-4   *Jn 20:2-8*

First Reading

On this feast of Saint John, we begin his first letter. We will examine the community that gathered around him which has been called the Johannine community. Their special experience of the Lord and Christian living is captured for us in this first reading. They probably lived in present day Turkey (Ephesus). It was a "rainbow" community composed of Jewish Christians, former followers of John the Baptist, some Samaritans and Gentiles. Their memories of the synagogues from which they had been expelled were bitter, hence their references to the "Jews"; their persecution by pagan governments scarred them, hence their references to the "world." Finally, they were wounded by internal dissension that broke out into open schism. This was the occasion for the letter of John. It is really a reflection on the experience of the Lord through a community tradition. In today's reading, John states that "we proclaim what we have seen, heard, touched and experienced" from the beginning. It was an apostolic experience which was proclaimed so that through hearing that Word later generations might have contact with the Lord. When we hand on a tradition, we are doing a great deal more than passing on facts about Jesus. We transmit their significance as well. Tradition is more than giving a crucifix to a child. It is taking the time to explain the meaning of the cross.

Gospel Reading

Peter and the "beloved disciple" ran to the tomb. They saw and believed: they realized the meaning of the folded garments and passed that meaning on to others. The Resurrection was not a visual event which anyone witnessed. However, after all Jesus had said and done, after all they had experienced in the passion events, Peter and the beloved disciple looked inside the tomb and saw the final clues that made the entire puzzle fit. The Lord is risen! To know that meaning is to have experienced the Lord. We keep this experience alive not only for ourselves but quite literally for the world. Without the Church, Christmas would long ago have degenerated into a simple "winter festival." We are the place where people can come to see what Jesus means, who Jesus is, what Jesus teaches and where Jesus gives life.

Point

People can find facts about Jesus in any library. We are the place where they come to learn the meaning of those facts.

DECEMBER 28
1 Jn 1:5-2:2   Mt 2:13-18

First Reading

A key word that helps us understand this Johannine community is "dualism." Throughout the Gospel of John and these letters, we see contrasts between freedom and slavery, life and death, truth and lies, good and evil, water and thirst, darkness and light. The phrase "God is light" appears some twenty-one times in John's Gospel. Light brings order into chaos and reveals an order that we never noticed was there. In the Johannine writings, "darkness" represents what is not God, not Christ — whatever is outside the Lord. It stands for chaos, ignorance or evil (Judas left when it was "night"; Nicodemus came "by night"). It is a multi-purpose word. The letter states that God is light and then describes those who broke away from the community. "If we say we have fellowship with God and walk in darkness, we are liars. If we say we never sin, we make God a liar." Evidently, the dissidents claimed an intimacy with God to the point of exonerating themselves of all guilt. It was an elitist exculpation of any wrongdoing because "God understands our reasons." In contrast, John states that Christian community is not essentially the absence of sin but the presence of repentance and forgiveness.

Gospel Reading

The Innocents were massacred in numbers that are unknown to us. Bethlehem was a small town and scholars suggest that thirty or forty may have been involved. The reference to Rachel crying for her children is very touching. Rachel had been the younger of Jacob's two wives. She was not as fruitful as the other wife and endured great ridicule for that. Finally, she gave birth to Jacob's two youngest sons, Joseph and Benjamin. When she died, she was buried at Ramah, north of Bethlehem. Centuries later, during the exile, the tribe of Benjamin was decimated and Jeremiah described Rachel as weeping for her children. Now, as the Innocents are slain in an area that used to lie within the territory of Benjamin, Rachel weeps again for her children. These children stand for all innocent people caught in the crossfire. Their presence during the Christmas season reminds us of another dimension of the Incarnation. With all the light the Lord has brought, the darkness is with us still.

Point

The pockets of darkness around and in us highlight the Light and show us the precise places it has yet to reach.

DECEMBER 29
1 Jn 2:3-11   *Lk 2:22-35*

First Reading

How can we tell whether our religious experience is real or phony? This first reading describes a bit more about that group that broke away from the Johannine community. They believed themselves to be so close to God that everything they did was excusable and rationalized in their own minds. In reply to them, the writer states that we know we have the spirit of Jesus by our observance of the commandments. Otherwise, any claim to an intense spirituality is a lie. We can be certain that we know the Lord if our conduct is like that of Jesus. This schismatic group evidently felt there was no connection between their outward behavior and personal religious experience. They assumed that their knowledge about Jesus immunized and deodorized everything they did. The message of John is that our daily actions are the best evidence of our faith.

Gospel Reading

The old man Simeon, who hobbled one day to the Temple, stands for the anawim, that small group of people who kept the spirit and the letter of the Law. This old man never wavered in his faith that God's word to Israel would come true. And it did — right before his eyes! To keep faith does not mean that we put our doctrines and religious practices in formaldehyde. It means that we live them out and hand them on by example. Faith is not simply an intrapsychic event. The real depth of our Christmas celebration is not found in the emotional surcharge we receive at Christmas but in its carryover into the days afterwards. If there is a real victory over darkness inside us by the Christmas light, it will show up in our behavior for all the world to see.

Point

The Word has to become flesh.

DECEMBER 30
1 Jn 2:12-17   *Lk 2:36-40*

First Reading

This first reading speaks about the "world" — a word that appears in the New Testament with two meanings. One meaning of "world" is the locus of redemption: "God so loved the world." The second meaning is as a symbol of darkness and opposition to God as in "the world, flesh and devil." In our own time, we know the world as the originator of the artificial heart, cancer cures, magnificent architecture, financing techniques, food distribution networks, the space shuttle, brilliant painting and poetry. This is also a world that houses abortion clinics, seriate marriages, gulags, drug traffic, ghettoes of every kind. These forces do a great deal of powerful preaching through the media. Such proselytizing is difficult to resist unless we have the power of God. John's point is that our baptismal Spirit is solidified by putting into effect Gospel living in our lives whether we be parents, children, professionals or retired people.

Gospel Reading

The prophetess Anna is the counterpart to old Simeon. She also stands for the anawim minority. They were a minority because the centrifugal force of the world is always drawing people away from God. It takes a great deal of strength and internal conviction to resist the world. These anawim did so because they opened their hearts to God, relied on the promise and dedicated themselves to covenant fidelity not only in large things but in small as well.

Point

Our Christian experience is strengthened in the world and in opposition to "worldly values" by keeping our ties with the Christian community strong. It is within the New Testament "anawim" that our faith is shared, celebrated and strengthened.

DECEMBER 31
1 Jn 2:18-21   *Jn 1:1-18*

First Reading

The Antichrist has always been a powerful symbol applied to a variety of political and military figures. John uses the word to describe those who have broken away from the community. It is a word of extremely bitter condemnation. It is clear that community cohesion in spirit and in truth was no luxury for the Johannine community at this critical period of their life. Schism could easily fragment and destroy this part of the Christian movement and weaken the love that should bind Christians together. In this light, we should see the enormity that John views to be embedded in what these breakaways have done. To separate themselves from the community was to segregate themselves from the Body of the Lord and to diminish their communion with the apostolic tradition. John encourages the remnant believers to stand firm in the Spirit they have received. The Holy Spirit within them is the conviction they are on the right track. Their corporate communion with the apostolic tradition is their assurance that they have followed truth rather than deception.

Gospel Reading

The famous prologue of John's Gospel from Christmas Day is repeated. This entire Gospel emerged from the same tradition and community that gave birth to the letters of John. Its themes and analytical tools are the same. The great overture to the Gospel that we find in this prologue sets out its major themes. The Word became flesh and blood; the Word continues to live among us; the Word is light and life for all that accept Him; opponents who have refused to share His life and love have chosen to continue to live in darkness.

Point

The world flickers with many lights. Only one of them can light up the darkness of mind and heart to expose the rest.

JANUARY 2
1 Jn 2:22-28   *Jn 1:19-28*

First Reading

Today's reading gives us deeper entry into the view of Christ espoused by the schismatic group that so devastated the Johannine community. "Who is the liar? He who denies that Jesus is the Christ." It seems that this group saw the Incarnation as little more than a subplot in God's dealing with mankind. God continues to do everything as He always did. Jesus' becoming man may have been beautiful and heart-warming but only an aside in the larger ongoing drama that continues undisturbed by it. John's response was an emphatic rejection of such a trivialization of the Incarnation. He asserts that the Incarnation was a major shift in our understanding of God and His ways. Christianity is not just the old time religion with a Christian twist. From now on, the best way to understand God is through the humanity, life and words of Jesus. Because of the Lord Jesus, we now realize that God works through humanity: people, emotions, intelligence and bright ideas — all informed by the Holy Spirit. God works as well through the humanity of the Church.

Gospel Reading

John the Baptist insists that he is only pointing the way to Jesus. Throughout the Gospels, John represents the old covenant, the prophetic tradition and all previous religious aspirations that predated the birth of Christ. This entire ensemble of theological and philosophical traditions all point to Christ. He is the full, final and normative expression of God.

Point

God is not simply found in the stars of the sky. Since the Incarnation, human beings are the principal instruments of God's presence in our world.

JANUARY 3
1 Jn 2:29-3:6   *Jn 1:29-34*

First Reading

The letter of John indicated that the Incarnation was not simply another option in our way to God. It is the paradigmatic way for all people. Today's reading looks at the same mystery from another angle. Because of the Incarnation, God now works through Jesus. The next step in the fulfillment of the Creator God's design is the communication of the Spirit of Jesus to each of us. We become sons and daughters of God by adoption and become capable of sharing life and intimacy with God as did Jesus. In addition, by virtue of our baptismal link with Christ, we can claim a share in the eternal life He possesses not through natural right but through baptismal right. This is a fact of faith that we do not fully appreciate. Our world is crowded with so many things that we tend to forget the presence of the Holy Spirit. We cannot see it, nor can the world see that Spirit. The Spirit, nevertheless, is there slowly changing, urging and moving us toward deeper unity with the Father.

Gospel Reading

Yesterday's Gospel reading carried John's disclaimers as to who he was not. Today, he tells us who Jesus is — the Lamb of God! The reference might be to Isaiah's lamb quietly led to death as the suffering servant. It might refer as well to the passover lamb of the Exodus which signified liberation from oppression. In either case, the point is that Jesus took away sin. He did not simply remove individual sins like objects out of a basket. Instead, Jesus defused the power of sin. He defanged and neutralized its power by giving us the new power of the Holy Spirit.

Point

The great sin is to deny the Holy Spirit in us.

JANUARY 4
1 Jn 3:7-10   *Jn 1:35-42*

First Reading

This first reading refers to the man who sins. It speaks not about the isolated, occasional wrongdoing of which we are guilty. John speaks about sin as a pattern of behavior. It is important that we not retroject our fairly elaborate anatomy of sin (mortal, venial, capital and cardinal) back to a time that saw sin as a way of living rather than a series of separable, individuated actions. "Sin" in the Johannine church was equivalent to lawlessness. The difference between our modern understanding of sin and that of John is that between a financial shortfall and bankruptcy; between the occasional burst of anger and viciousness. It is a sinful pattern of living that reveals a person to be without Christ.

Gospel Reading

In this reading, the Baptist's followers begin to follow the Lord. Discipleship is more than formal church membership or the memorization of teaching. It is living as Jesus did. Faith is not a set of individuated acts so much as it is a pattern of living. We follow the Lord not by showing an occasional charismatic gift but by fidelity, concern and prayerfulness as permanent features of our personal landscape. The pattern of Christian living shows us to be followers of the Lord more than do spurts of religious feeling. Like the disciples, we spend our lifetime trying to follow the Lord through the novel fact patterns that repeatedly break into our lives.

Point

Learning to follow Christ is a "hands-on" experience and the heart of the Christian adventure.

JANUARY 5
1 Jn 3:11-21   *Jn 1:43-51*

First Reading

We have a practical application of the life of the Spirit in today's first reading. John gives us two examples of ways of living. He contrasts the murderer Cain with the self-sacrificing love of Christ. These diametric opposites are the magnetic poles toward which our lives are attracted even though we do not completely imitate either one. Our love can take many demonstrative and subtle forms. Our hate, as well, can take many direct and indirect forms. We are presented with the contrast to appreciate the fact that our lives are gradually being drawn toward Cain or toward Christ.

Gospel Reading

A number of titles are given to Jesus: Rabbi, Messiah, the One described in the Law and Prophets, Son of God and King of Israel. The evangelist is telescoping a number of crystallized insights about the identity of Jesus into this little scene only to show them all to be partial. Jesus tells Philip that a point will come when he will see heaven and earth meet — that is, he will come to see the deeper meaning of all these time-honored titles. In the same way, our understanding of Christ, of discipleship and of what Christian love requires do not occur in a flash.

We come to such realizations over times both good and bad. As our own lives and personalities unfold, we see more layers of meaning in time-honored doctrines and memorized words of Scripture. Events can release depths that we never quite appreciated before. We can come to realize, over time, the power and permutations of sin as well.

Point

The events of our life do more than bring us new information from the outside. They enable us to experience the Spirit we carry within with new power.

JANUARY 6

1 Jn 5:5-13   *Mk 1:7-11*

First Reading

This cryptic reference to the water and the blood is an arresting and vivid image. Jesus came not only in water — that is, John's baptism — but in blood as well, through His passion. Faith is more than a generalized trust in God. It is a specific understanding of God's ways as shown to us in Jesus. Only such a specific faith gives eternal life and a share in Christ's risen life. What we believe makes a difference. The "conqueror of the world" is not just a person who believes deeply any religious proposition. It is a person who believes Jesus is the Son of God. The letter is asserting that John's baptism of Jesus — the rush of the Spirit — was important but incomplete. The Word became flesh but the ability of Jesus to communicate His life to others occurred on the cross — in the blood. When water and blood flowed from His side, He handed over the Spirit. The saving power of Jesus is available to us not only through the

Incarnation but through the Incarnation as completed and fulfilled by His saving death and Resurrection.

Gospel Reading

The events surrounding John's baptism of Jesus are recounted in this Gospel reading from Mark. It sets the tone of the life and ministry of Jesus. It is a compact action. It capsulizes the moment when Jesus realized His mission, accepted that mission, submitted to the Father's will and was accepted by the Father. It concentrates the entire drama of the life, death and Resurrection of Jesus that had to be played out. It was baptism, confirmation, ordination and anointing all in one. The effects of this moment would be made real in the months and years to come. On Easter Sunday, this brief episode received its full and final meaning.

Point

Baptism, Eucharist and Spirit were symbolized in the dove, water and blood. The sacraments are now the ways that Jesus transfers His life to us.

JANUARY 7
1 Jn 5:14-21 *Jn 2:1-12*

First Reading

The "deadly sin" is mortal sin or more accurately, deadly sinfulness. It is activity at total variance with our calling as Christians. The Johannine community saw the reception of Baptism and the Spirit of Christ as a new birth. A person received a new principle of action and life from which there

might be minor deviations but the thrust of an individual's life
was Godward. If a person lived the opposite kind of life, it
evidenced not the impotence of the Spirit but personal resist-
ance to the Holy Spirit of Christ. If a person has set himself on a
deadly path, no amount of prayer can convert such an individual. Our prayer can result in inspirations, opportunities,
movements by the Spirit. In the end, however, such an individual must receive the Spirit and submit to His control. In the
face of refusal, the Spirit will not operate. The only force that
can impede the saving power of Jesus is not a satanic one. it is
human indifference.

Gospel Reading

The wedding at Cana provides the occasion for the first of
Jesus' signs in John's Gospel. Commentators have found all
sorts of meaning in the wedding setting. Symbolisms that have
been suggested are nuptial, Marian, sacramental, covenantal
and creation-affirming. We have the old water of Judaism
turned into the new wine of Christianity; the bonding of Jesus
and the Church; the covenant love of marriage blessed by the
Lord all suggested by this scene. Together with the first reading,
we can use the Cana incident as a model of the union of a
person's spirit with the Holy Spirit in Baptism. Like a sacramental wedding bond, that union is indissoluble. We never have to
be rebaptized whatever our sin. Just as one spouse can ignore
the other and be unfaithful to their bond, so we can ignore and
be unfaithful to the Holy Spirit who is bonded to us.

Point

*The binding of the Spirit to us in Baptism, like the marriage
bond, is no assurance of our lifelong fidelity. It is the starting
point for great spiritual success or failure.*

MONDAY after Epiphany
1 Jn 3:22-4:6   *Mt 4:12-17, 23-25*

First Reading

Dealing with and discerning spirits comprise the subject of today's first reading. Whether we try to discern the source of the spiritual movements we feel within us or try to place some order into the array of emotions and feelings that crowd our lives, the need for criteria is critical. Discernment is never facile. A person can experience inspiration without its origin being from the Lord. Conversely, an individual can experience a sense of unworthiness and yet be a person of great faith. Religious emotions do not carry credentials of their authenticity of place of origin. John suggests that we must import criteria to test the spirits. The feeling of love for God must be backed by our behavior. Emotions of devotion are no substitute for concrete charity. Further, Christian experience as distilled in Church teaching is another guide. During times of emotional disorientation ("How can it be wrong when it feels so right?") the teaching of the Church is a reliable yardstick.

Gospel Reading

Jesus moves from Nazareth to Capernaum to begin His public ministry. The Baptizer had set the stage and now Jesus begins to build the kingdom with a message similar to that of John: reform to prepare for the kingdom. This message remained the essence of Jesus' teaching. His entire ministry was built around this fundamental message: change because the power of God moves among you. Reform was the precondition for reinstating that deeper, easier, liberating communion with God that had been lost in the distant past of our species and which Jesus singularly possessed. He was calling people to a more abundant life in the free flow of God's Spirit through them. In His ministry, Jesus was able to discern spirits of illness, possession, grief, hostility and material attachment. His openness to the Father enabled Him to clearly discriminate among them.

Point

God reveals Himself through the inner workings of our minds. It is important that we learn to discern what is from God and what is not.

TUESDAY after Epiphany
1 Jn 4:7-10   *Mk 6:34-44*

First Reading

The word "love" appears so frequently in the New Testament writings attributed to John that he has been called the apostle of love. Over centuries, love has received many definitions in sexual, romantic, patriotic, commercial, social and religious contexts. The love of which John speaks in today's first reading is a giving love. It is not the love of self-absorption in which a couple excludes the world to celebrate their emotional attachment to each other. It is not the love that gives itself to extract an exclusive return. The love God has for us was given its most vivid expression in Jesus who gave His own life as a trade for our own. It was freely given not through any desert of ours but out of His generosity. It was total. This is the kind of sacrificial love John suggests as a model for Christian love. It is neither devoid of, nor equivalent to, emotional attachment. It is sacrificial.

Gospel Reading

In a scene heavy with eucharistic overtones, the Lord feeds the hungry people. This action of Jesus is a parable in drama in which, anticipating His eucharistic gift of Himself, He feeds His followers from His own power and thereby gives an example of service. His gift turned a crowd into family. They are no longer isolated disciples but a congregation assembled on this hillside to hear His word and receive His bread. This scene continues among us not only in our eucharistic celebrations but also in our relationships toward each other.

Point

Christian love gives rather than takes.

WEDNESDAY after Epiphany
1 Jn 4:11-18   *Mk 6:45-52*

First Reading

In this first reading, John writes that although we cannot see God optically, we can know Him from the effects of His presence, one of which is love. How we get from the presence of Christian love to the presence of God is based on the example and work of Jesus Christ. Where the kind of love Jesus showed to us is present, He assured us that He would be there as well. His love and peace are the empirical effects of His new invisible risen presence. The message of the Incarnation is that because of our baptism, human love and concern can embody the risen Lord. We are now the secondary causes through which His presence continues to make itself known throughout the human community.

Gospel Reading

The storm in this reading is more than just a windstorm. The early Church Fathers saw it as a symbol of the storm that beset the early Church and individual lives as well. The incident reveals that Christ is with us in the storm. The episode concludes with the strange line that they "did not understand about the loaves." Its meaning is that the disciples did not understand this new manifestation of divine power that adumbrated the Resurrection presence of the Lord. They failed to see that there was a spiritual presence of Christ, as in the Eucharist, that cannot be seen visually but which has its effect through human initiative and love. Jesus is as present among us with this new spiritual presence as He was with the disciples in the boat.

Point

We have the power to actualize and project the risen presence of the Lord through the assistance we give to others.

THURSDAY after Epiphany
1 Jn 4:19-5:4   Lk 4:14-22

First Reading

There are many ways of showing love. There are also many ways of watering down the Christian concept of love. We should not forget that love, any love, has real power. Love is not just a personal sentiment descriptive of our reaction to another person. It has real power to revive others, to release them, to reveal God and to restore people to wholeness. So often in our own experience, we have known individuals who seem to find a new lease on life, a new reason for living, once they realize that they are loved by another. It shows them that they are valuable. All the more can Christian love restore to others a sense of self-worth not only as objects of affection but as sons and daughters of God with an irreplaceable purpose in the design and kingdom of God.

Gospel Reading

The Lord reads from the prophet Isaiah in the only Gospel reference we have to His having read anything. This section of Isaiah announces the periodic year of grace and jubilee of the Old Testament in which debts were forgiven and the slate was wiped clean. It has come into the Christian Church as the Holy Year. These very words have become a charter for theologies of liberation in which the Gospel brings not only spiritual freedom but also liberation from oppressive social, economic and political structures. In our context, it refers most radically to freedom within. The Lord came to release us from all the forces that can paralyze our ability to speak the truth, live justly and love thoroughly. This is the more radical and personal kind of liberation that frees us from the power of sin. It unties whatever holds us in bondage and releases the power of the Holy Spirit.

Point

It is an important personal moment when we realize that we are not just liked, tolerated or appreciated but loved by God.

FRIDAY after Epiphany
1 Jn 5:5-13   *Lk 5:12-16*

First Reading

More important than human testimony is the testimony of God. John's Gospel and the Johannine church placed great emphasis on the legal function of a witness. In a court of law, witnesses can be called to testify to the veracity of Jesus' words and promises. Throughout His life, Jesus had witnesses: the Father was witness at His baptism; the works He did were corroborations of His message. The final witness referred to in today's first reading is the water and the blood. The sacrificial and saving death of Jesus was the final testimony to the authenticity and reality of His message, claim and life. The water and the blood are powerfully graphic and dense symbols of the sacramental life of the Church. For us who have not heard the Father's voice at the Jordan, who have not seen firsthand the miracles of Christ, we have the sacramental experience of the Church in which we encounter the risen Lord through the rituals and community of the Church. For us, that is a powerful witness to the Lord's risen life.

Gospel Reading

The works Jesus performed in His lifetime are really continuations and expansions of His prophetic message. Jesus showed that He came not only with words but in power to let loose into the world His lifegiving Spirit to continue His healing and preaching work. Leprosy in the Gospels is extremely evocative. His curing of lepers represented a mission to outcasts, to those swollen in pain, to those the law cannot cleanse, to people at the margins of society. The Incarnation was not just to be material for a delightful nativity scene. That mission of

Jesus remains an imperative for us. We are all called to break down those humanly imposed divisions among us and open the structures of our society and Church to the life-generating power of the Spirit.

Point

Both the disease of sin and the power of Christ are progressive and radical in their effects.

SATURDAY after Epiphany
1 Jn 5:14-21   *Jn 3:22-30*

First Reading

The first letter of John concludes with today's first reading. After a letter that spoke of the great gift of life and love we have been given in the Lord, the writer closes with a reminder that we should pray. It is part of Christian love to pray even for those who have sinned and departed from the way. The gift of discerning God's presence and love that we have been given is not to be hoarded and kept. We are to share that gift with others. If people refuse to listen to us, we can still pray to the Father for them that a power stronger than our own can reach into that innermost part of themselves to smash the chains that prevent them from moving forward into a communion with fellow Christians.

Gospel Reading

This odd scene portrays Jesus as baptizing. It is not a question of sacramental baptism as we know it. Most probably, Jesus and His disciples were continuing the bath of repentance that John had initiated. Some of John's disciples remark that the people seem to be flocking to Jesus to receive the ritual immersion. John's reply restates his final message that his function was only to point the way. He compares himself to a best man at a wedding whose role is simply to bring bride and groom together. John had done his best to prepare the people of Israel for the Messiah. He had pointed out the Lord, called for repentance. Now, the chemistry between Jesus and the Jewish people would have to take over. The same is true of ourselves. We work to link people with the Lord. We can only do what is within our power and then let the chemistry between the Holy Spirit and individual hearts take over. Just as the Baptist was not responsible for later Jewish rejection of Jesus, so we cannot hold ourselves responsible for those who refuse to accept the Lord.

Point

Prayer remains the first and last resort in our efforts to bring others to the Lord.

LENT and EASTER

ASH WEDNESDAY
Jl 2:12-18; 2 Cor 5:20-6:2   *Mt 6:1-6, 16-18*

First Reading

The word "Lent" comes from an Old English word for "Springtime" — a season when new life is wrested from the clutch of winter. Lent is our time for revival and renewal — the springtime of the spirit.

We have all been through enough Lents to realize that complete transformation probably will not occur. But Lent is an opportunity for repair work in a specific area of our life that might need reconstruction.

Maybe you have doubts about the faith or questions about things we do as a Church. Lent is a time to resolve the doubts and get some straight answers.

Maybe you have been carrying personal wounds that have been eating away at you. Lent is a time to find ways to let the healing begin.

Maybe your spiritual life is stuck in neutral and you want to be able to pray as easily and spontaneously as Jesus did. Lent is a time to start to experience prayer.

Each of us has some part of our life that needs a lift and some remodeling. Lent is less a time for pain and punishment than it is a time for healing. As Joel says in today's first reading: Nobody is exempt. Call everyone together — priests, lay people, young and old. This is the levelling significance of the smear of ashes: beneath all our differences, we all need renewal.

How do we start? One way might be to arrange to talk for a

while with a priest or another fellow-Christian, or with the family.

Another way might be to select a book carefully. There is a great deal of good writing on every area of life and concern to Christians. Be sure, however, it is a book with a size and style with which you feel comfortable.

Also, so that our Lenten resolutions do not disintegrate as our New Year's resolves may have, we might share what we have chosen to do with someone else. We can then encourage each other.

Lent is not a time for temporary improvement until Easter after which we go back to business as usual. Its purpose is to make a lasting change in our life. If that is something about which you have been thinking, Paul says in today's second reading that "This is it!" This is the time! Right now! The iron is hot!

In the Gospel reading, the Lord reminds us not to go through the motions alone because this is serious business.

If you are willing to undertake this effort and to experience through your Lenten resolutions the death and Resurrection of Christ, I ask you to step forward to receive these ashes, ancient symbols of penance and renewal. Please come forward as we all begin to walk together this very personal road from winter to spring, "from ashes to Easter."

THURSDAY after Ash Wednesday
Dt 30:15-20   *Lk 9:22-25*

First Reading

The theme of choice dominates today's readings. The reading from Deuteronomy was probably used at the annual covenant renewal ceremony in ancient Israel. It portrays in stark fashion the choice with which we are presented: life or death, God or idols. That choice was made not only by a single generation of Israelites. As the Old Testament so graphically depicts, it was a choice made by every generation. We make that same choice as well. It is not only a choice that we constantly make as individuals. It is also a choice made by every community, generation and nation. It is individual and collective as well. If we have chosen the way of the Lord, we are required to live, often enough, in an era that has chosen otherwise.

Gospel Reading

The Lord asks what profit there is in gaining the entire world if a person destroys himself in the process. There are ways in which a person can stop and look at the direction in which his or her life has been going.

Religious practices are one indicator. The frequency of our eucharistic celebrations, Scripture reading and prayer time tell us a great deal about the condition of our spiritual life. Lent is also a time to see what we do with our religion. Prolonged introspection can often reveal within us only what we want to see. Another method is to examine the pattern of our relationships with others. If we see a series of harmonious or acrimonious interactions, we discover a great deal about ourselves. It will exhibit the thrust of our life rather than isolated moments. This is one step in a productive Lent in which we can take an honest look at ourselves.

Point

If we look at the direction of our life, we will be able to see whether, in the words of Moses, we have been choosing life or death.

FRIDAY after Ash Wednesday
Is 58:1-9   *Mt 9:14-15*

First Reading

Isaiah describes dysfunctional fasting, a fast that went bad. Instead of deepening the life of the Spirit, it choked it off. The result was not unlike that of placing 200 smokers in a room together two weeks after they have begun to give up smoking for Lent. Chaos! Danger! Isaiah points to the deeper purpose of fasting which is not only self-control that liberates the spirit, but awareness of the human need that surrounds us.

Gospel Reading

The Lord refers to fasting as a way of deepening our spiritual experience of the Father and Son. Since the Lord is physically absent from among us, fasting is a way of reaching deep down within toward God.

There were three focal points to Lent in the Roman tradition: prayer, alms, fasting. Lent is the great time of prayer — not necessarily more prayer as much as better prayer. There are various kinds of prayer that can bring new vitality and repose to our communion with God. Almsgiving is basically sharing. It is more than the sharing of money. It can involve an extension of our time, our life experiences or our spirituality to others. Almsgiving reminds us of a broader world and lifts us from the narrow compass of our problems to the wider world of wrenching need around us.

Finally, fasting is much more than dieting. It means eating, drinking, smoking less. Its purpose is to enable us to regain control over our appetites, something that is especially difficult in a consumer-oriented society. If we cannot control our bodies, we will find it extremely difficult to control our spiritual selves. The effort to fast reminds us how closely we are tied to bodily gratification. It seems to be a part of universal wisdom, East and West, that fasting is vital for spiritual self-mastery.

Point

A careful, methodical observance of Lent enables us to learn something about ourselves, about others and about God.

SATURDAY after Ash Wednesday
Is 58:9-14   *Lk 5:27-32*

First Reading

This reading from Isaiah of Babylon was written after the destruction of Jerusalem and continues his great poem begun yesterday about the true purpose of fasting. Isaiah reminds us that no spiritual or ritual exercise can tie us closely to God if we are torn apart from our fellow human beings. It is tempting during Lent to select a series of personal spiritual exercises which we can perform privately and individually. We expect that faithful adherence to this spiritual regimen will yield a more profound spirituality. Isaiah tells us (and every age) that the adjustment of our lives with others, the hard work of reconciliation and seeking some small measure of equity is the true starting point for a heightened sense of God.

Gospel Reading

The Lord calls Levi and then dines with an entire parliament of tax agents. He refuses to treat them as pariahs. Even if they had been an especially corrupt group, which they probably were not, their continued isolation and de facto excommunication would have done little to change them. Hence, the Lord insists on exchanging fellowship with them that they might witness His teaching put into practice even though they might have otherwise been reluctant to hear it expounded in theory. Our own lives can provide a more powerful attraction to the unchurched and alienated Christian than would any lecture or homily. The power of example is gigantic. We preach what we practice.

Point

The solid base on which our spiritual efforts of Lent should be grounded is the effort to heal our relationships with others.

MONDAY — First Week of Lent
Lv 19:1-2, 11-18   *Mt 25:31-46*

First Reading

The Book of Leviticus is an expansive commentary and application of the Ten Commandments. It applies the desert code to a bewildering variety of situations resulting in a combined religious, civil and criminal code. To understand the rationale of each of its provisions takes us very deeply into the heart of Israelite life. The decalogue contains the minimal requirements of God's law of civilized behavior. They evolved largely as a series of prohibitions stating what should be avoided. Even the affirmative commandments devolved into a list of itemized prohibitions. That approach is clear in today's first reading. The thrust of the Decalogue is not yet love. It seeks justice first.

Gospel Reading

In the parable of the sheep and goats, the Lord tells His disciples how the nations will be judged. Even those who were never acquainted with any specific word of God, who had not been exposed to the Gospel, remain bound by obligations both moral and natural to their fellow human beings. This parable reminds us that the Lord calls us to do more than the minimum. We are to seek out affirmative ways of loving and caring.

Two distortions can throw a healthy sense of sin off-balance. The first identifies sin almost exclusively with sexual sin. The word "immorality" comes to connote only sexual and venereal excess. Yet, the scope of sin embraces economic, environmental, commercial and nuclear kinds of sin. The second distortion identifies sin with doing evil. But we can sin and "miss the mark" by failing to do good. The Lord reminds us in today's Gospel reading that neutrality can be a sin. We can harm others and break the covenant by doing nothing.

Point

During this first week of Lent, we might consider whether our spiritual life is mainly geared toward avoiding sin or whether it centers on seeking ways to reach others to do good.

TUESDAY — First Week of Lent
Is 55:10-11 *Mt 6:7-15*

First Reading

This reading from Isaiah of Babylon praises the power of God's word. It has an inevitable effect. If disregarded, it becomes a word of judgment. If that word is allowed to be planted within us, it will bear fruit to an unexpected extent.

Gospel Reading

The Lord gives the disciples an example of how they are to pray: with economy, trust and intimacy with God. Like making love, prayer is one of the things we all have to do on our own. Nobody can do it for us. Speaking with God is an intensely personal event. Lent is usually our annual attempt to improve our prayer life in some way.

There are two extremes that make prayer difficult. The first confuses prayer with our daily routine. Prayerful living is not identical with prayer. If getting through the day is the extent of our prayer life, prayer loses its distinctive character. The opposite extreme identifies prayer exclusively with surges of mysticism. A rapid pulse and wild transports of spiritual passion are not attractive to many people. There has to be a middle ground between the two. This is what the Lord describes.

We should have a set time for personal prayer. In addition to our regular prayers, we should find a time when we are most at ease to simply communicate with the Lord and not be interrupted by anything else. Some people even set aside a place of prayer in their homes. Secondly, our prayer should be authentic. There is no need for us to posture before God or recite prayers written by a great saint which we think God will like to hear. Thirdly, we should await the Lord's response. After a while, we will not be greeted by silence. We will slowly tune in to the Holy Spirit.

An important meaning of the Lord's Prayer is that we can contact the God of the universe. Reading a great deal about prayer is not initially helpful. Like teaching, litigating, preaching, driving or swimming we have to start at some point and will improve slowly. After several months of experience, books will be more helpful.

Point

Through prayer, we locate the still point inside ourselves. When we locate that point, there we will find the Spirit of Christ.

WEDNESDAY — First Week of Lent
Jon 3:1-10   *Lk 11:29-32*

First Reading

To mention Jonah is to think of the whale. But the Old Testament book has a different and more significant point to make. After the scene in today's first reading, in which Jonah preached repentance, everybody repented. The next verse tells of Jonah's displeasure and anger. The Book of Jonah is an indictment of Judaism's narrow focus. It criticizes a view of the covenant that sees it as limitative of God's love — as though God and Israel were going steady and neither could even look at another.

Gospel Reading

The Lord refers to Jonah as the most important sign the Pharisees will receive. It is not the credentials of Jesus that should be an object of meditation. It is His message. Just as the Ninevites did not ask for Jonah's resume but saw the truth of what he said, so the call of Jesus to return to the true meaning of the covenant should suffice for the Pharisees. If they fail to see the significance of His teaching, an examination of His credentials would not help. We do not have to check the academic background of someone who tells us that infanticide is wrong. The truth of his message should be obvious to all but the most degenerate.

An honest self-examination is a significant Lenten attainment and a critical juncture. It enables us to know where to direct our spiritual energy so that we are not simply spinning wheels for Lent. Also, it is possible to rationalize sin away and become immune to the Gospel message. If we are able to sense the need for change in our lives and to locate some snags and shortcomings, that, as with the Ninevites, is a sign of spiritual life. It is a sign that God cares and that His love does in fact surround us.

Point

The sense of sin means that Easter for us is really possible.

THURSDAY — First Week of Lent
Est C:12, 14-16, 23-25   *Mt 7:7-12*

First Reading

The story in the Book of Esther takes place in Persia (Iran). One of the king's anti-semitic advisors planned to exterminate all the Jewish people. Esther, a Jewish woman, pleaded with the king for her people. Through her charm, beauty and intelligence, the Jews were spared. This deliverance is celebrated today as the Jewish holiday of *Purim*.

In this first reading, Esther prays to God to deliver her people. God does deliver them through Esther. He answered her prayer in a way that she did not expect. When we pray, God answers our prayers, not necessarily through direct and miraculous intervention, but through the instrumentalities of other people as well as our own abilities.

Gospel Reading

The sense of the Lord's words in the Greek language of the Gospel is to keep on asking, to keep on knocking and to keep on praying. This is not a recommendation to bombard heaven since the Lord told us not to rattle on and on in prayer. Rather, He asks us to keep the attitude of prayer so that we can recognize the answer when it comes in an unconventional guise. Prayer attunes us to discern God's response in the events of our life. Perhaps we limit the kind of response we expect God to give to our prayers. When it is answered in a way different from what we expect, we can fail to recognize it.

Point

If we keep the attitude of prayer, we will find that the Father does answer us in His own way — as He did answer the prayer of Esther.

FRIDAY — First Week of Lent
Ezk 18:21-28   *Mt 5:20-26*

First Reading

Both of today's readings are about conversion. This first reading from Ezekiel is a major breakthrough in Old Testament prophetic thinking. For the first time, Ezekiel underscores individual responsibility in contrast to collective grace and guilt. There may be such a thing as community sin and community grace which is more than the sum of its parts. Communal sin and guilt has a dimension that is not simply additive but geometric. Just as the holiness of the Church is more than the sum of its saints, so communal morality has a supervening existence of its own in which we share. Ezekiel's message, however, is that, although we may be responsible for the society in which we live, each of us stands before the Lord on our own two feet. We cannot blame our parents and society for the evil we do or for the good we fail to do. Each of us is held to account for our own lives.

Gospel Reading

The Lord speaks about reconciliation with one another. Reconciling with enemies is not an easy thing to do. Yet, the Lord's words remain for us. If we bring a gift to the altar and recall a distance between ourselves and others, leave the gift and proceed to horizontal reconciliation first. Our worship should reflect the life we live.

Such a single act of reconciliation can be the most difficult thing we do during Lent. That one effort can be more demanding than any amount of fasting and spiritual exercise. In fact, many of us would prefer penitential rituals than approaching another to say, "Look, we cannot go on like this!" It is far easier to seek reconciliation with God than with other human beings. But when two people do put down their weapons, both of them are changed. Such reconciliation can be a moment of grace and growth. If we are changed by injury, then we are transformed by forgiveness as well.

Point

If we can bring ourselves to forgive or be forgiven by another, this Lent will have been a success.

SATURDAY — First Week of Lent
Dt 26:16-19   *Mt 5:43-48*

First Reading

The final instructions of Moses to the people remind them of their special place as God's own people and of the gift of Law they have been given. The Torah Law was given to Israel as a prescription for national unity, moral coherence, prosperity and happiness. The historical difficulty lay in the repeated disregard or dilution of those laws. Therein lies the story of mankind's failures as well as its moments of glory.

Gospel Reading

The Lord tells us to love our enemies. Love of neighbor carries its own burden of difficulty. That difficulty is cubed when we try to show love to the very people who have tried to do us in. The Lord is not asking us to carry a warm glow of affection for those who are trying to destroy us. He is referring to the obverse of retaliation. At some point, we have all experienced the twinge for revenge. Usually, after we have had an opportunity to regain perspective, that feeling may have departed. It was the instinct to strike back. The Lord is telling us to do the very opposite. Whenever we respond to those hostile to us, we should do so in terms that will help that person dissolve his or her hostility. A wan smile will not achieve that. In fact, if an individual rages at us with fury and we respond with a calm and modulated voice, that can be a subtle and cunning kind of retaliation. The Lord indicates that our response to the conflicts that bubble up in our lives should be geared to the good of the other individual. He tells us to pray for those who are against us. As Christians, we must always be conscious that we are followers of Christ even in our conflicts.

We are expected to do more than react instinctively in con-
flictual situations. We are called to bring perspective to human
affairs and to respond as representatives of the Lord.

Point

*Through dealing with conflict, we will slowly be perfected
to become like our Father in heaven and our Lord on earth.*

MONDAY — Second Week of Lent
Dn 9:4-10   *Lk 6:36-38*

First Reading

As we begin this second week of Lent, today's reading
comes from deep within the heart of the Jewish exile. It is
Daniel's act of contrition on behalf of the nation. His prayer for
pardon is predicated on the fact that all have sinned. We all fall
short of the glory of God. We too have departed from our
baptismal promises. In varying degrees, we all have not obeyed
the Lord's word to us. We are reminded that we should be
looking critically within ourselves and at our lives during this
penitential period and not primarily at the behavior of others.

Gospel Reading

The Lord declares that our method of measuring others,
our standards, tell us a great deal about ourselves. How we deal
with other people is an index of our spiritual health, of our
image of God and of the Church. None of us has a microscope
powerful enough to enable us to peer into the soul of another
person. Almost by necessity, we see only externals — the
surface of another's motives, intentions, and thoughts. The rest

is surmise or guesswork. For this reason, the Lord warns us not to judge, condemn or lack compassion.

Our attention should turn to ourselves for an examination of our conscience. Lent is a time to place ourselves before a crucifix to review our life, our personal story of sin and grace: what we have loved, whom we have loved, how sensitive or insensitive we have been to God's grace. Doing so before a crucifix has a serious rationale. We are to compare ourselves not with other people but with Jesus Christ. We are called to be imitators of Him and to put on the mind of Christ. He is our model. We are not to gauge our superiority or inferiority to those around us. There is no growth in that. The Lord Jesus is our standard.

Point

The awareness of God's abiding presence is the result of the conjunction of our spiritual discipline and God's gift.

TUESDAY — Second Week of Lent
Is 1:10, 16-20 *Mt 23:1-12*

First Reading

The prophets are easily caricatured as doomsayers and nothing more. They are often popularly portrayed as purveyors of an angry message from an angry and arbitrary God: Do this — or else! In today's first reading, Isaiah speaks to the southern kingdom of Judah, a much more conservative people than was northern Israel. He describes a people whose social fabric was rent. The notion of covenant living with its implication of fair dealing and mutual assistance was gone from the national ethos. Dramatically enough, he compares Judah to Sodom and

Gomorrah in its rabidly individualistic gluttonies. His message to them is that unless they begin to redress these massive social inequities, they will become flaccid and a prey to a stronger, internally coherent aggressor. What Isaiah describes is a religion that has lost its soul. The people of Judah were simply going through the motions.

Gospel Reading

The Lord also describes a religion that has lost its soul. The formal teaching of the Torah Law remained valid. It was God's revelation and gift to Israel. The Lord criticizes the elaborate customs and conventions that grew up around the Torah. Florid tassels, marks of honor, elaborate displays were in evidence while the main point of the Torah Law — covenant living — was neglected in practice. External practices, therefore, are not the whole story of religion. They are the husk that carries within it a spiritual treasure. Faith cannot survive if it is never given expression. We cannot "love Jesus in our heart" and never show it. Faith is not an exclusively mental event. Isaiah denies such a privatization of faith. The question for Lent is whether we translate our faith into visible behavior. Are we more compassionate, more willing to listen, more patient with others? Here, at our eucharistic celebration, we are disciples of the Lord. When we leave the church, we become apostles. People do not see Christ anymore. They see us.

Point

There can be no such thing as a "secret disciple."

WEDNESDAY — Second Week of Lent
Jr 18:18-20   *Mt 20:17-28*

First Reading

Jeremiah was another southern prophet who spoke near the end of Judah's political life. His message was almost synonymous with doom and gloom. He spoke against king, clergy, sexual abuses, and hypocritical Temple worship — thereby successfully alienating all the major sectors of Judah's establishment. In this first reading, his enemies are plotting to eliminate him. The temple priests, the local wise men or commentators and the paid prophets gather together. We have Jeremiah's prayer in which he asks God whether it is just that a man who has only obeyed God's command should be so treacherously repaid. The unwillingness of the people to listen and the hatred they displayed toward him were the suffering he bore. Legend has it that he was exiled to Egypt where he was put to death. The early Church saw him as a model of Christ.

Gospel Reading

For the third time, Jesus predicts His coming suffering and death. A Jewish mother interrupts to ask that her sons get a short cut to glory. Jesus' response is that there is no short cut to spiritual glory or spiritual life. We cannot bypass the cross. Suffering can take many forms in our life. It can be a recognition of our personal limitations — we simply cannot do or be anything we would like. It can be the suffering that comes from dull routine. It can take the form of our inability to change or reach certain other people. It can be our frustration with ourselves and the realization that personal change is not as facile as self-help books suggest. The spiritual value of these sufferings derives from our making them an integral part of our spiritual life rather than denying or refusing them. When we do that, we become less judgmental of others and less perfectionistic in our expectations. If we adopt the attitude of the Lord, we will see our suffering not as a penalty but as a service to our brothers and sisters.

Point

Suffering is not a detour or mistake but our unique way of serving the Lord.

THURSDAY — Second Week of Lent
Jr 17:5-10   Lk 16:19-31

First Reading

Lent forces us to examine where we place our trust. In today's first reading, Judah is on the edge of national disaster. Jeremiah reminds king and royal court not to place their basic trust in alliances or the word of foreign officials but on the covenant. The national disregard of the covenant was a spiritual leukemia eating away at the very lifeblood of the nation. This reading raises the question for us as to where we look for inner security, peace and forgiveness. In Jeremiah's time, the people looked to every place except covenant living. They replaced the personal bond of the covenant with tricky and transient political alliances.

Gospel Reading

The Lord's parable of the rich man and poor man makes the same point. Wealth or poverty is not an automatic index of spiritual strength or emptiness. The point is that financial success does not imply spiritual success. Academic achievement does not imply spiritual insight. The accumulation of property does not imply that a person has developed powerful inner resources. The rich man is condemned not because he was rich but because his wealth had made him indifferent to the plight of others. Lent is a time to become realistic about our relationship with the Lord. Otherwise, when the things on which we rely fail and are taken from our life, we will discover too late that we have nothing deeper upon which to rely. We will have fooled ourselves. Lent is a time to make an experiment and put aside a number of ordinary diversions in our life to explore where we stand with the Lord.

Point

We should not look to things for something only God can give: inner healing, strength and peace.

FRIDAY — Second Week of Lent
Gn 37:3-4, 12-13, 17-28   *Mt 21:33-43, 45-46*

First Reading

The story of Joseph, the dreamer, is a familiar story from our Bible history days. He had quite a few offensively self-centered dreams that his father Jacob loved but which drove his brothers to distraction. They could not endure his endless recounting of them nor his favored status with their father any longer. They sold him into slavery. Joseph became so adept at dream interpretation in Egypt that he became an economic advisor. The early Church saw Joseph as a symbol of Christ. He was betrayed by his own and then raised to glory. What looked like defeat was turned by God into victory.

Gospel Reading

In this pivotal parable, the rebellious tenants reject the prophets and Christ. What looked like defeat was turned by God into victory. It was the start of a new covenant and a new people of God from a stone kicked aside by the original builders.

Dreams play an important part in the Bible and an important part in our lives. They are a safety valve, the origin of our great ideas, refreshment for the mind and the playground of our unconscious. They show that there is much more depth to us than we think. There is a great deal more going on within us than that of which we are aware. This is also the level at which grace works. Deep inside us is where the mysterious symbiosis between God's love and our free will grows. Just as the Joseph story shows that God is woven into seemingly secular events, we can personalize the Gospel parable to say that God can take our sin, our failures, and turn them into instruments of renewal.

Point

There is much more going on in our life with God than we know.

SATURDAY — Second Week of Lent
Mi 7:14-15, 18-20   Lk 15:1-3, 11-32

First Reading

The southern prophet Micah gives a resume of God's continual care for the people of Israel and Judah. He recounts the deliverance from Egypt and the willingness of God to forgive and wipe the slate clean. This ringing affirmation of God's love is often accepted by us in theory. It is much more difficult for us to accept the fact that God forgives our sins forever. Once He has forgiven, He carries no grudges and does not dredge up past faults to double our burdens today. Frequently, our scrupulosity and guilt reflect an unwillingness to forgive ourselves and to accept God's forgiveness. Viscerally, we seem to be more ready to accept a vengeful God who exacts a price for every sin than to believe in a God whose forgiveness flows freely.

Gospel Reading

In one of the most moving parables of Luke's Gospel, we are given a story of human sin, divine forgiveness and restoration and human resentment. The spendthrift son is welcomed back gladly and fully. The father runs out to greet him and to restore him to the place he deserves without recrimination or revenge. The elder son resents the benign treatment the younger son receives and the seeming obliviousness of the father to the enormity of the spendthrift's sins. On one level, this is a parable of the Gentiles and tax collectors welcomed by Christ into the circle of God's love in a way resented by official Judaism. On a more personal level, we can place ourselves into the place of any of the parable's characters. At times, we have been the wasteful son. We also have been the forgiving father who overlooks many wrongs. We also play the part of the elder son resentful of the ease with which some people are forgiven without seeming to suffer any hardship for their sins. These three figures capture important moments of salvation history. We have all played each of these roles. The Lord uses this story to teach us that forgiveness, and not revenge, is alone capable of making people whole again.

Point

Forgiveness heals. Retaliation shifts resentment onto a different plane.

MONDAY — Third Week of Lent
2 K 5:1-15   *Lk 4:24-30*

First Reading

The pagan Naaman makes a double appearance today. He had been a powerful commander in the Syrian army. With all of his wealth and clout, he had one problem — leprosy. The traditional horror of this disease derived from its appearing to make the sin of the soul visible on the skin. Lepers were seen to be especially punished by God. Naaman had heard of Elisha (Elijah's successor) as one who could possibly cure him. He came prepared for fireworks and bizarre rituals but was told instead to do something very simple — to wash in the Jordan. He was insulted by the instruction to do something so trivial in a river that was dinky and ludicrous by Syrian standards. Eventually, he followed instructions and was cured. The point is that the power of God effected the cure. Obedience to His Word was the operative event.

Gospel Reading

In His maiden sermon in the synagogue, Jesus refers to the cure of Naaman to show that God's love is universal. At that, the local Jews were ready to kill Him. They ejected Him from the synagogue. Ecumenism was not a major element of Judaism in that era. The Lenten point we can draw from this episode has to do with the ritual simplicity of forgiveness. During this time we consider the tragedy and horror of sin; we then are told that to have sin forgiven we have only to repent and confess. An act of confession takes about five minutes and yet, with that, all our sins are gone forever. It may seem too simple. If sin is as horrible as we are told, we should have to suffer, sweat and bleed for the forgiveness we receive. But Someone has already suffered, sweated and bled in our place. This also is the message of Lent.

Point

In the act of confession, we become as acceptable and lovable in the Father's sight as we were on the day of our baptism.

TUESDAY — Third Week of Lent
Dn 3:25, 34-43   *Mt 18:21-35*

First Reading

The first reading from the Book of Daniel recounts the prayer of Azariah, one of the three young men to be sent shortly into the fiery furnace. It is a prayer from people in exile without leader, priest, prince or prophet. It is a prayer that God accept repentance and sorrow — the only things the people have left to offer. As it turns out, that was always the best thing they could possibly offer.

Gospel Reading

Today's Gospel reading delivers a powerful parable about the meaning of forgiveness: seventy times seven, says the Lord. In the previous section, the Lord described fraternal correction. He spoke about dealing with a member of the community who is stubborn in his or her wrongdoing. His words describe a preliminary form of due process through an escalating set of corrective steps. The question then arises not about a stubborn member but an individual who simply makes quite a few mistakes. How many times must we forgive in such a case? The Lord says that we should forgive all the time. To illustrate this, He tells the story of a huge debt forgiven for a servant who then refuses to delay repayment of a much smaller amount owed him by another. The point is that our readiness to forgive others should be patterned on our experience of God's forgiveness of our sins. If our readiness to forgive will benefit another and restore a relationship, we should be always ready to do so. It is the only way to break the constant recycling of anger and revenge.

Point

The test of how truly we accept God's forgiveness is our willingness to forgive others.

WEDNESDAY — Third Week of Lent
Dt 4:1, 5-9   *Mt 5:17-19*

First Reading

Today's particular selection of readings is very old. It goes back to the ancient practice of using the period of Lent for the final preparation of catechumens for Easter baptism. This third week was devoted to the commandments and Law. As we can see from today's first reading, the Torah Law for the Jews was the most complete and precise expression of God's will they had. They revered that Law and enshrined it in a special place of honor in their synagogues. Law, any law, puts the conscience and highest aspirations of a people into words. It gives expression to the most profound and vital values that animate a culture. In the Torah Law, God put into words, throughout Israel's history, the vision of what the people of Israel should be. For this reason, law is never trivial or discardable.

Gospel Reading

For this reason as well, the Lord states emphatically in today's Gospel reading that He did not come to abolish the Law but to fulfill it. He came to draw out its real meaning. In the section immediately following today's reading, we have the Lord's litanic repetition, "the Law says, but I say. . ." The commandments remain God's word and are holy. But the spiritual perfection and depth the Lord brings requires that we go further than the Law. If we measure ourselves against the standard of the Law, it is easy to become self-righteous. Most of us do not steal, commit adultery or murder. If we place ourselves against the standard of Jesus Christ and the Law He announces in the Sermon on the Mount, our own life is thrown into stark relief. This sermon throws a floodlight on every part of our life as we realize how far short we fall of the mark. The Lord calls us to more than legal compliance. He invites us to spiritual perfection.

Point

Obedience to the Commandments is not the end product but the starting point of the Christian life.

THURSDAY — Third Week of Lent
Jr 7:23-28   *Lk 11:14-23*

First Reading

In yesterday's reading, the Book of Deuteronomy mandated respect for the Torah Law. Today's first reading from the prophet Jeremiah gives us the rest of the story. Through Jeremiah, God addresses His people to tell them that in fact they had never listened to or obeyed that Torah Law. They were always in some stage or phase of rebellion against it. They had turned their backs on it. They knew God's will but did not follow it.

We are often told that if people know what is the right thing to do, they will do it. We know this is not the case. We are not purely rational animals. Some evidence for this is found in the habit of smoking despite authoritative warnings that it is harmful to human health. Lent is not an intellectual exercise in which we try to acquire more information about the moral life. It is a time to learn to control our desires and to let God's Spirit transform us.

Gospel Reading

The Lord tells the brief parable about the strong man able to guard his house until a stronger appears and enters to steal the owner's weapon. As long as we are in control of ourselves, the power of evil is weak. When our will and minds weaken through our assimilation of attitudes and practices that are not Christian, we surrender the most valuable weapons we have in our journey of Christian growth. Our strength against evil derives from renewed hearts and minds and not from any book or piece of information.

Point

The struggle of Lent is not simply against the devil and the forces of evil. It is also with parts of ourselves that have not yet been sanctified by Christ.

FRIDAY — Third Week of Lent
Ho 14:2-10   *Mk 12:28-34*

First Reading

Hosea was a prophet to the trendy northern kingdom of Israel. This group of Jewish people were much more willing than Judah to assimilate pagan practices. For their syncretism, they were taken over by the Assyrians and deported much earlier than was Judah by the Babylonians. Hosea looks past the Assyrian takeover to a time of healing. He describes an era when the people would return to God with minds and hearts made new. He looks to a time when the renewed people of God would worship with their whole heart, soul and mind — something which Israel had never done and was, in fact, powerless to do.

Gospel Reading

Asked which of the Jewish laws was the greatest, the Lord responds with two quotations. He refers to the Deuteronomic command to love God entirely and to the injunction from Leviticus to love our neighbor as ourself. Both of these references expressed ideals. The Lord's surprise equation of them was innovative. The rest of the New Testament and Church history is an effort to apply those commands and keep them in balance. At times, one receives more emphasis than the other. But the dynamo of the Christian life lies precisely in the continuing search for balance between piety and social justice. Both sides bring their own kind of fulfillment. Times of prayer as well as times of reconciliation can be deeply rewarding. Lent is a time to again seek a balance. If our spiritual life is marked by a deep love of God and prayer, Lent is a time to reach out to our neighbor. If our spirituality is marked by deep involvement with others, Lent is a time for more personal and intensely private prayer. Keeping these two moments in balance is the engine of the Christian life.

Point

The very act of trying to balance love of God and of neighbor enlarges us and draws us closer to Christ.

SATURDAY — Third Week of Lent
Ho 6:1-6   *Lk 18:9-14*

First Reading

Transient piety does not bring an abiding spiritual fulfillment. This is the message of Hosea. He speaks both to the northern (Ephraim) and southern (Judah) kingdoms. We come to appreciate the vacuity of sin and false piety when the security structures we build collapse and we see our spiritual safety to lie in the Lord alone. "On the third day, he will raise us up" is one of the prophetic statements fulfilled on Easter. It has a more immediate historical reference here. The piety of the people had been like the morning dew, superficial and easily burned away. The Lord responds to this religious attitude that had grown up over the years by saying that He desires love and knowledge of Himself more than sacrifices and charcoal burned carcasses. (These words were quoted by Jesus). The Lord seeks a realistic recognition of our need of God as the premise for our restoration to peace and prayer.

Gospel Reading

Neither of the two men in the parable were evil. The Pharisee kept the law he was instructed to observe. The exact fulfillment of the regulations blinded him to the need we all have of God and further growth in the Lord. He saw no further distance he had yet to travel. He was complete, finished, fulfilled. He had reached the end of his spiritual trail. The publican, or tax agent may or may not have kept all the legal prescriptions. His profession was one that made him personally hated and ritually unclean. He realized his need of God. The Lord points to him as the one who left the Temple that day enriched spiritually and closer to the kingdom.

Lent is less a time for us to focus on all the evil of which we have been capable and perhaps guilty than it is a time for us to search out ways we can improve and draw ourselves more closely to the Lord. It is a time not only for avoidance of sin but for entering into a deeper and more fulfilling spiritual life.

Point

We seldom grow spiritually by only looking backward. We should look forward to what we can be in the Lord more than to what might have been.

MONDAY — Fourth Week of Lent
Is 65:17-21   Jn 4:43-54

First Reading

In this first reading, we have a second (possibly third) prophet we call Isaiah. The first Isaiah spoke a word of judgment before the exile. Now, the exile is about over as Babylon collapses and another Isaiah writes about the future. When this other prophet spoke about going back to the old days, he describes a second Genesis, a new creation: new heavens and a new earth where infants will not die young and old people will live to see the fullness of their allotted days. "Look, I am doing something new." His message is that the great acts of God are not limited to the past of Moses, to the Exodus or to David. He looks forward to a great future act in a person we call Jesus through whom God will intervene in a brand new way to start a new creation. Lent is not a time to try to turn back the clock. God can use our past to lead us to a deeper experience of Himself. The great acts of God for us are not confined to the past.

Gospel Reading

Jesus restores an official's son to health. John sees this as the second great sign Jesus worked. In John's Gospel, all of Jesus' signs are heavy symbols of what He is doing on the deeper spiritual level. They are parables of sacramental experience. John shows that there is no difference between the original eyewitnesses and ourselves in terms of our ability to experience the Lord's transformative power. The deathless Christ, the Jesus of Easter, becomes part of us in the Eucharist. We can draw strength, power and vitality from His Resurrection right now. Our life here is not a dress rehearsal for eternity. We are presently living God's life which trajects through death and explodes into eternity.

Point

The spiritual life must be more than a constant look back. God is with us in the now.

TUESDAY — Fourth Week of Lent
Ezk 47:1-9, 12   *Jn 5:1-3, 5-16*

First Reading

This strange vision from the end of the Book of Ezekiel shows a small trickle that becomes a gigantic torrent. It symbolizes the life that would come from the restored Temple as a spiritual influence after the exile. It refers as well to the Church which starts small and grows into a great and holy people of God. It refers also to the waters of Baptism which give life to the Church and to new members as the simple pouring of water becomes the source of the great company of saints throughout the world. We can apply the point of Ezekiel's vision to our spiritual life. Our growth in holiness starts in small things. Nobody is a mystic overnight. We begin with everyday acts of charity and slowly we grow. We cannot leapfrog into dramatic Ezekiel-like spiritual visions and experiences.

Gospel Reading

This cure is the third of Jesus' signs in John's Gospel. As always with John, it is a great deal more than a cure. The emphasis of the incident is not on the water but on the healing. Jesus delivers a long discourse afterwards in which He explains that this healing is only a symbol of the kind of life He gives. The Lord brings not just more biological life but a spiritual energy that binds all the different levels of our life together. He states in verse 21 that just as the Father raises the dead to life, so the Son gives life to those who are alive now.

At the beginning of Lent, we indicated that it was important that we take one area of our life and deal with that manageable portion rather than trying to effect total change. Such small success is an important foundational experience for later growth. Even a huge, rushing river has to start somewhere. A magnificent, power-filled spirituality has to begin with fidelity in small things. It is in those smaller areas where we should expect the healing power of Christ to first penetrate to spread throughout our lives.

Point

We must attend to sound beginnings. The more solid the start, the more authentic will be what grows from it.

WEDNESDAY — Fourth Week of Lent
Is 49:8-15   *Jn 5:17-30*

First Reading

Today's first reading from Isaiah of Babylon was written during the exile as it was about to end and the signals of a chance to return home were on the horizon. While Judah was in exile, many questions arose in her national consciousness. The people questioned why this tragedy had struck them. They had certainly done wrong but in comparison with pagan cultures they were relatively devout. They looked again at the covenant with David, heralded as an everlasting pact. They had come to interpret it as a guarantee of political invincibility. Now, it seemed that God had abandoned them. Isaiah's message was that God had not left them. He offers a vision of restoration not to the old Davidic days but toward a new future. He looks forward to a spiritual and universal kingdom. The exile was to be a time of transition. Isaiah's message is that God was not finished with Judah at the end of David's reign. That was just the start.

Gospel Reading

The Lord gives a sermon after the healing of the crippled man. He speaks about His closeness to the Father and asserts that the Genesis Sabbath did not signify the termination of God's work. The Father continues the work of creation through the Son. As with Judah, the ministry of Jesus showed that God was not finished with the world. We can apply this to ourselves. Spiritual growth should not be interpreted as though at some point in the past we had reached a perfect state, the outer limit of our spiritual growth, then fell away and have been trying ever since to return to that moment. Just as our emotional and psychological development do not end at the age of "maturity" so our spiritual life continues to mature as well. The growing pains, crises and periods of spiritual exile we endure all indicate that the Lord is not finished with us. That will happen only on the day we die. Until then, we experience the shaping, molding, growing and deepening.

Point

We cannot stop the changes of our life. The issue is whether we will allow God to shape us through those changes.

THURSDAY — Fourth Week of Lent
Ex 32:7-14 *Jn 5:31-47*

First Reading

Moses spent too much time on the mountain and the people below began to go astray. They settled into a way of life oblivious of their special deliverance by the Lord. God instructs Moses to return to his people because they have become

depraved. Moses prays for God to avert any punishment from
the people for their sin. The prayer of Moses saved the people.

Gospel Reading

The Lord speaks to Jews who refuse to believe in Him.
Their accuser is not Himself but Moses. Jesus fulfilled all the
promises and goals of the covenant. This refusal to accept Him
stems from a deeper hardness of heart. During this second half
of Lent, we should remember those who have forgotten or
neglected this period of grace. As much as those who are
physically ill, they need our prayer.

When we pray for others, there is often a delayed action in
its effect. We do not see immediate results. In praying for a
change of heart in others, we are dealing with something
extremely intricate — human free will. When we pray for the
Holy Spirit to let others see the light, the result could be
mechanically insured if people were puppets. But they are not.
Just as sin, to be sin, must be conscious, intelligent and free, so
the act of faith, to be faith, must be conscious, intelligent and
free. Robots can neither sin nor believe. Through our prayer,
God will inspire, illumine and present opportunities to others.
In the last analysis, they must make the act of faith. This is
precisely what the Jews in the Gospel refused to do. The
opportunity, freely given, was rejected. As long as there is life,
there can be revived faith. However far a person may seem to
have drifted from the Lord, we should not abandon them. God
does answer our prayers for them. The question is whether
they, in turn, will answer God.

Point

*Everyone can be affected by our prayer. They must re-
spond, however, to those effects.*

FRIDAY — Fourth Week of Lent
Ws 2:1, 12-22   *Jn 7:1-2, 10, 25-30*

First Reading

This wisdom reading, written about a century before the crucifixion, describes the thinking of people who are opposing a mysterious just man. We do not know exactly who he was. It is a picture of the true Israelite whose life quietly puts into stark relief the lives of those around him. He is very much like the righteous man of the Psalms and the mysterious suffering servant of Isaiah.

Gospel Reading

The Gospel readings from this point describe the growing tension between Jesus and His opponents. As we approach Holy Week and Good Friday, various programs will appear in the media discussing the circumstances of the Lord's passion and death. There will be several interpretations of motives: prejudice, orthodoxy, fear of political unrest, self-interest, politics, jealousy and hatred. The events of Holy Week submit themselves to differing legal, political and sociological analyses. We must remember that beneath all of these, the fundamental conflict is between the power of God and the power of evil, between sin and grace that is taking place in the life and body of Jesus. Evil can be seen from different angles but it remains evil. It was not politics, treachery or the quantity of pain that was the spiritual turning point of our redemption. It was Jesus' obedience to the Father. Paul tells us that Jesus was obedient even to the point of crucifixion. It was because of Jesus' obedience that He was exalted at Easter and became the source of life and power for us. As the Church Fathers were fond of saying: Jesus reversed the disobedience of Adam. Jesus' obedience turned the politicking, self-interest, betrayal and pain of Holy Week into a saving sacrifice that bought back a world.

Point

The conflict between good and evil takes various disguises. Through the Lord, we can make our immersion in that conflict redemptive for ourselves and others.

SATURDAY — Fourth Week of Lent
Jr 11:18-20   *Jn 7:40-53*

First Reading

Jeremiah is embroiled in a plot against his life which he is powerless to prevent. For a life of preaching God's word, he is now held to account by a group of self-seeking and arrogant people. Jeremiah's single prayer is for divine vindication. He can only submit to the meshing of gigantic forces arrayed against him and hope that the God who gave him life and a mission will rescue him. He prays in a prayer found so frequently in the Old Testament for the opportunity to see God's vengeance upon those who have so wickedly plotted against him. He wants to see them paid back in spades.

Gospel Reading

Jesus is also embroiled in controversy. The people who knew little of the intricacies of the Law were attracted to the Lord. Those who had steeped themselves in the Law and knew the names of every tree while missing the contours of the forest refused His message. He seemed not to fulfill a specific item of prophecy. The Messiah was to have been born in Bethlehem. Jesus was from Nazareth. They refused to hear His words. The ordinary people heard the word of the Lord while the Pharisees spent time flyspecking His credentials. Soon, this almost comic opposition will become more violent and brutal. The significant difference between the Lord and Jeremiah is in their response to opposition. Jeremiah prayed for revenge. Jesus will beg for the Father to forgive. There can be no clearer indicator of the difference between the testaments and the completeness with which Jesus expressed the best of the Law and prophets in His final cry for forgiveness for those who crucified Him. That was the final authenticating sign, the ultimate credential of His origin. It was what prompted the Gentile officer, who also knew nothing of the intricacies of the Law, to say that this truly was a son of God.

Point

The Spirit of Christ can transform our reactive instincts into vehicles of spiritual growth.

MONDAY — Fifth Week of Lent
Dn 13:1-9, 15-17, 19-30, 33-62   *Jn 8:1-11*

First Reading

This first reading from the Book of Daniel was written several generations before Christ about a story placed back in the time of the exile. It is a tale embroidered to make a point. It shows God's justice at work. Susanna had been falsely accused by some judges whose minds were not on true judgments but on other things. She is saved in the nick of time by Daniel whose adroit cross-examination saves the day for her. It is a straight story of good and evil. Injustice is opposed here to justice. The deeper message embedded in this story is that God's justice and fair dealing among people do not simply happen. God's justice was accomplished here through the intelligence of Daniel. We have to work to bring about fairness for those people who, for any of a number of reasons, have ended up with the short end of the stick. We are instruments of God's justice. But justice is not the whole story.

Gospel Reading

The Lord goes a step beyond justice in today's Gospel reading. Susanna was innocent. The woman here was a certified adulteress — "caught in the act." Here, the leaders want to do justice and follow the Law. The Lord goes beyond Old Testament Law toward forgiveness. For a long time this incident was in a Scriptural limbo because Jesus was seen as being too soft on sin. It travelled among Gospels, dropping out of some manuscripts, popping up in others, until it finally found a home in John's Gospel. It really is a lesson against dumping on others. Self-righteousness is always a temptation. There are outrageous sins and crimes. But behind that wrongdoing is a person. There is a great deal more to a sinner than the sin which he or she commits. That is the part which the Lord reaches out to touch.

Point

Our sense of justice should be tempered by Christian common sense and care.

TUESDAY — Fifth Week of Lent
Nb 21:4-9 *Jn 8:21-30*

First Reading

In this enigmatic incident from the Book of Numbers, the people are healed by looking toward the symbol that incarnated the poison that infected them. By God's power, and not by the simple looking, they were healed.

Gospel Reading

The running debate between Jesus and the Pharisees continues. There is a kind of resident obtuseness or lack of sight in their understanding of the Lord's words. He states, "When you lift up the Son of Man, you will come to realize that I AM, . . . I say only what the Father has taught me."

On the cross it all comes together. The cross is perhaps the central devotion of Christian spirituality. If we could point to any one symbol that captures everything Jesus was and is, everything He said and did, it would be the crucifix. The cross contains all kinds of meanings. It says a great deal about mankind and about God; it says a great deal about love and about hate; it says much about sin and about grace. It is as though all the parables, healings and discourses of the Lord imploded into the cross and Christian thinkers have spent centuries drawing that meaning out. We bring our own meanings to the cross as well. It is the one constant in our lives from the time we were children. It is no surprise that the crucifix has a central place in all Christian churches. Like the bronze serpent which Moses raised in the desert, it is at once a symbol and an instrument of healing. Generations of Christians have looked to the cross as the most dramatic and profound symbol of the meaning of Christ. It freezes the moment of death, of human excess and, as John's Gospel emphasizes, the moment of new life as Jesus hands over the Spirit.

We can take some time during Lent to exercise our spiritual sight and look at our lives in the light of the cross. It is the perfect image of God's love and of the reach of human love as well.

Point

The real meaning of love is shown by the cross.

WEDNESDAY — Fifth Week of Lent
Dn 3:14-20, 91-92, 95   *Jn 8:31-42*

First Reading

At last, we have the story of the three young men in the fiery furnace. They are called Hananiah, Azariah and Mishael in Hebrew or Shadrach, Meshach and Abednego in Babylonian. This is an exile story. King Nebuchadnezzar was a particularly vicious conqueror. Before he blinded the Jewish king Hezekiah, he had his son killed before his eyes so it would be the last thing Hezekiah would ever see. He built a 90 foot idol and expected everyone to worship it when the band played the proper song. When the tune was played out, everyone knelt except three Jewish civil servants. To punish them, he has them placed into a superheated furnace. They are seen to be protected by an angel of God. Nebuchadnezzar converts and issues a new order that those who do not worship the God of Judah will be torn limb from limb. Conversions are indeed gradual. The story really tells more about the later years of the Maccabean period than about the exile. Its universal point is that God freed the three because of their faithfulness.

Gospel Reading

The Lord speaks about freedom at a very deep level. A person who lives in a free country is not necessarily free. Freedom is, most profoundly, a matter of the spirit. We can be chained by habits, compulsions, prejudices and sins that make any political freedom we might have illusory. The Lord says that everyone who lives in sin is a slave. Freedom comes from faithful trust in God. The Jews retort that they have faith from Abraham. Jesus responds that faith is not in the genes; it is an act a person makes on his or her own. Simple descent from Abraham does not make an individual a believer. Faith is a personal act.

A Catholic education is not the whole story. At some point, we must make an adult act of faith in which we embrace our heritage. Lent is a time to examine not only our adherence to Catholic practices and doctrine but to see how deeply and personally we have made that faith and its tradition our own.

Point

It is not the doctrine about Jesus but the Lord Himself who will set us free.

THURSDAY — Fifth Week of Lent
Gn 17:3-9   Jn 8:51-59

First Reading

In this first reading, God promises Abraham the whole land of Canaan as a permanent possession. This promise has been highly politicized in the volatile atmosphere of the Middle East. Its biblical import is not political but spiritual. The descendants of Abraham saw themselves as a chosen people based on this promise and God's covenant with Abraham. It was a special distinction. Abraham had a revered place in Jewish tradition as one especially chosen by God for divine favor.

Gospel Reading

We can see the great touchstone of holiness and promise that Abraham was among the Jewish people in this controversy with the Lord. Jesus speaks about the eternal life that He makes available. As always in John's Gospel, the Jewish leaders speak to the surface level of things and events. They discuss chronological age. Jesus was not yet fifty. Abraham was long dead yet Jesus claims to give eternal life in a way superior to anything that Abraham ever had. Finally, Jesus makes an assertion that was tantamount to blasphemy when He says that before Abraham ever was born, I AM. Jesus applied the great and mysterious Exodus name of God (Yahweh = I AM) to Himself in the clearest and most direct identification of Himself with God that was conceptually and linguistically possible among Jews. We Christians share in Jesus' fulfillment of the Old Testament tradition. We are His chosen people. Our chosenness and spiritual life do not occur in a vacuum but are situated. We live in a particular city, with a particular set of family relationships and with a particular line of work. None of these is irrelevant to our chosenness. Our special responsibility as God's people is modified and influenced intrinsically by the circumstances of our life.

Point

We show our special link with God by how thoughtfully and uniquely we follow our Lord.

FRIDAY — Fifth Week of Lent
Jr 20:10-13   *Jn 10:31-42*

First Reading

The scenes in these two readings are seven centuries apart but they are very closely linked. Both Jeremiah and Jesus brought God too close for comfort. In this first reading, Jeremiah did more than disturb the status quo and say unpopular things. He rocked the theological foundations of the dynasty. He criticized the popular Davidic theology which came to see God's covenant with David as an invisible protective shield. Jeremiah insisted that the covenant was a mutual responsibility. God would protect the people if they followed the rules of covenant living. In the welter of the political chaos that engulfed Judah at this time, Jeremiah saw the judgment of God. By seeing the presence of God's work in secular events, he brought God too close to home.

Gospel Reading

The Jewish people had come to see God as majestic and remote. There is a comfort in that. If God is so distant, we can justify ourselves in not living according to His will. Jesus insisted that God is majestic but not remote. The implication of this is that everything we do, sacred and secular, has spiritual and therefore eternal consequences. There is a spiritual dimension to our everyday life. As a result, our spiritual life cannot be repaired or improved independently of the rest of our lives. In fact, our spiritual life is a reflection of the rest of our life. The meaning of all this is that God is inserted very deeply into our life. As one great theologian said, the mystery of God is deepest within us and the furthest from our manipulation.

Lent will conclude in a few days and some questions arise.

Have we come to a greater discernment of God's will for us during this Lent? Have we discovered some unknown areas of darkness and of unexpected light in our lives? The real mark of a holy Lent is the difference it makes in our lives after Easter.

Point

Sin and grace affect not only our souls but our entire being.

SATURDAY — Fifth Week of Lent
Ezk 37:21-28   *Jn 11:45-57*

First Reading

This first reading from the end of the Book of Ezekiel speaks of the coming restoration and kingship of David. Ezekiel speaks of the reign of Christ. He could only express this prophetic insight in categories and language that were familiar to him. He speaks of David as the new, faithful and enduring Prince of the people. The great sanctuary, restored and rebuilt, which will last forever is the great Emmanuel and not any building. The covenant which will endure forever is the risen humanity of Jesus that forever bonded mankind with God through the Holy Spirit. Within a culture and time of the Old Testament remote from our own, Ezekiel is really describing Easter Sunday.

Gospel Reading

The plot against the Lord is hatched and set in motion. This very effort to destroy Jesus would be the instrument of His transformation into the Risen Lord who would rule a kingdom deeper, wider and more enduring than anything that Judaism could have anticipated. Just as Caiaphas spoke words whose full import were unknown to him, so the planned destruction of Jesus would end the reign of the old covenant and open the kingdom of God to all people. The prerogatives so jealously guarded by these high priests would be cancelled and a new outpouring of God's favor would be given to those who believe in the very person they were attempting to destroy. In this piece of plotting, ancient forces and ancient enemies are slowly coming together for the great battle about to take place not on the field of Esdraelon but on the hill of Calvary.

Point

Exile and death give birth to new and vigorous life.

MONDAY of Holy Week
Is 42:1-7   *Jn 12:1-11*

First Reading

On Monday, Tuesday and Wednesday of Holy Week, the first reading is from one of the Suffering Servant songs found in Isaiah. Each of these songs refers to a mysterious suffering servant of God; each of them gives us a different insight into his soul. Some have said the servant is the Jewish people in their national torment of exile; Israel as God wanted her to be; some holy man Isaiah knew; Isaiah himself. The Christian tradition has always seen these poems as referring to Christ. The servant in Isaiah's prophecy became an instrument of God not suddenly, but through his suffering. Hence the name, Suffering Servant.

Gospel Reading

The Gospel reading about Mary's anointing of the Lord's feet refers to His death and burial. In this reading, almost as an aside, John seems to want to show that Judas did not become a traitor overnight. It was a long time in coming. In the same way, we cannot isolate this Holy Week from the rest of the Lord's life. Holy Thursday and Good Friday are not independent from all the parables, healings and teachings of the Lord. In fact, this Holy Week will show the real meaning of everything that has occurred up to this point in Jesus' life.

In our lives, every success and every setback can be an opportunity for deepening faith or it can be left unused. Our ultimate act of worship is what we do with our lifetime. Everything that happens to us can enrich that worship or simply be left to the side. Isaiah's suffering servant used his life experience in one way; Judas used his in another.

Point

Saving power is not intrinsic to the events of our life. It is something we bring to them.

TUESDAY of Holy Week
Is 49:1-6   *Jn 13:21-33, 36-38*

First Reading

Today's reading from Isaiah speaks about the mission and destiny of the mysterious Suffering Servant whom the Church identifies with the Lord Jesus. "The Lord called me from birth to be a light to the nations." It is a great destiny. But then Isaiah adds his further words, "Though I thought I had toiled in vain and for nothing. . ." He was not certain where it all fit into the divine plan. He believed that God would somehow draw it all together.

Gospel Reading

In today's Gospel reading, we have an odd collection of characters: Peter professing loyalty, John asking questions, Judas going his own way. God used all of them, even the traitor, in bringing about redemption. God pulled it all together. Today, we consider the place of our lifetime in the majestic perspective of God's work in our world. Each person's life is an important fragment of God's design even though we might not presently be aware of our place in that plan. To those willing to listen, God speaks through events. He speaks in the great events of salvation: Bethlehem, Calvary, Easter Sunday, Pentecost. He speaks in the extraordinary events of our lives: births, deaths, marriages and illness. He speaks in our daily life situation. Our life is a constant spiritual unfolding of ourselves to God and of God to us. We all should know more about ourselves today than we did during Holy Week a year ago. We should also know more about God's will for us than we did last Holy Week. If we consider things that occurred to us a few years ago whose purpose was puzzling, they are probably no longer as deeply mysterious to us. Through our daily life, God's will slowly becomes clear if we take the time to listen and discern His voice.

Point

Though I thought I had toiled in vain and for nothing, uselessly spent my strength, yet. . .

WEDNESDAY of Holy Week
Is 50:4-9   *Mt 26:14-25*

First Reading

The suffering that saves can take many forms. The holy Servant of God in today's first reading describes two moments in his life. The first is his reading, meditating and assimilating the word of God. "Morning after morning he opens my ear that I may hear." The word of God became so incarnated in him that he learned the possibility of redemptive suffering. The second moment arrives when he puts that meaning into practice as he endures the hatred and rejection of those who oppose him. In the face of their hate, his faith comes to the fore as he realizes that God will be his ultimate vindicator. Our knowledge that suffering patiently endured has saving power does not remove the sting of suffering but can enable us to bring God's love even to those who oppress us.

Gospel Reading

The sufferings of Jesus did not begin on the cross or in the garden of Gethsemane. More than the thorns and nails were the sufferings of abandonment, rejection and betrayal. The fact that these are psychological does not make them any less real. In today's Gospel reading, we have the Lord at table with His closest friends. These were the ones with whom He shared everything He was and hoped for. Yet, even from them, one would rise and leave to betray Him. We cannot but feel that pang of sadness which stabbed Jesus' heart when He heard the door close and heard the steps of His betrayer hurry on their mission. More than any physical pain, the rejection and refusal of people to accept His love was hurting to the Lord. We have no reason to believe that such pain in the Lord is over. He has indeed risen and no thorn or nail can harm His risen and transformed body. But the pains of refusal and rejection remain. In this sense, the passion of Christ continues in our own day.

Point

Even the suffering that Christ endures now is being transformed into an ongoing redemptive moment.

EASTER MONDAY
Ac 2:14, 22-32   *Mt 28:8-15*

First Reading

After the great celebration of Easter, further remarks seem anticlimactic. Several points emerge from today's readings. In this first reading from the Acts of the Apostles, we see the start of a theology of Christ. The Apostles had experienced the Risen Lord and, after Pentecost, they began to comprehend and explain its meaning. Their first turn is to the Old Testament in whose light they interpret the life, death and rising of Christ. Peter remarks in this Pentecost sermon that God was at work from the very start in everything that happened to Jesus. Jesus was not just lucky. It was part of a design. The treachery, denial and pain were all ingredients of God's saving purpose.

Gospel Reading

These Resurrection appearances of Christ show that He had a real body. He was not a vision, dream or hallucination. People in those days were familiar with the differences among such phenomena. These appearances emphasize the identity of the earthly Jesus of Nazareth they all knew with the risen and transformed Christ. Strangely, Jesus seems to break off meetings during these appearances. Their purpose was to strengthen a faith that was already there. They are not meant to stop the clock and encourage disciples to venerate the empty tomb. Rather, these appearings propel them to share their faith experience, to move outward from their small community to others as they spread and preach news of the kingdom that has been born with Jesus. The disciples would come to have differences among themselves but their common experience of the Risen Lord would give them a framework in which to see their problems.They would come to realize that their difficulties were a reliving of the passion, death and Resurrection of Christ. Our liturgical experience of Holy Thursday, Good Friday and Easter provide a framework in which to locate all the other events of our life. That experience should also propel us outward to strengthen faith, share faith and begin to establish the kingdom.

Point

We provide the connection between the Resurrection event and our world.

EASTER TUESDAY
Ac 2:36-41   *Jn 20:11-18*

First Reading

We see a developing Christology in Peter's Pentecost sermon. In preaching the meaning of the Resurrection, Peter

asserts that God made Jesus "Lord." We use that word automatically without adverting to the powerful significance it had
for Jewish people. It was an exalted title that was translated as
Kyrios in Greek. The Greek word meant "master" or "lord" as
used for nobility. It was also a pagan title for their gods. It was
the word used by the Greek Old Testament for "Yahweh."
Therefore, to call Jesus "Lord" was to give divine honors to
Christ. It was a drastic step for Jews. Most important, the use of
this title for Jesus was not the result of a gradual development
but was virtually instantaneous with the experience of the
Risen and Transformed Christ. It came from the apostolic realization that now Jesus rules, Jesus forgives, Jesus strengthens us
with word and sacrament. "Lord" meant that Jesus had a
special and unique relationship with the Father. Additionally,
He was Lord of everything. The life of Jesus was seen as being a
great deal more than a local Jewish event. Now, they saw that
everything Jesus said and did had universal significance.

Gospel Reading

The words of Jesus to Mary Magdalene can be either
translated as "Don't touch me" or "Stop touching me." The
translation, "Do not cling to me" captures the point. The
Resurrection meant that Jesus had a new relationship with
people that was deeper and more intimate than was possible in
Galilee. The Risen and Transformed Christ was now the glue of
this new community of faith. The Church was composed of
those who were changed by their experience of Christ. Later
generations would be exposed to a similar experience through
their own dying to sin and rising to new sacramental life. As
Peter declares in today's first reading, we can experience the
saving power of Christ by our repentance and baptism. In that
way, we can internalize the dying and rising of the Lord.

Point

The Church is composed of those who can repeat the words of the earliest creed from the depths of their own experience that "Jesus is Lord."

EASTER WEDNESDAY

Ac 3:1-10   *Lk 24:13-35*

First Reading

How and where do we meet the Risen and Transformed Christ? The theme of these readings is the continuity between Jesus of Nazareth and the Risen Lord as well as between the Risen Lord and the Christian community. In this first reading we see the healing ministry of Jesus continued by the Apostles. After the Resurrection, Jesus did not perform any healing miracles. He now operates through the community He created. Although we can obstruct that ministry, He continues His work today through us if we let Him.

Gospel Reading

This reading brings us closer to the purpose of the Resurrection appearances of Christ. With the Resurrection, Jesus became the universal Christ. He is everywhere slowly urging and moving our world toward a point of convergence with the Father. There are points where this Risen and Transformed Christ is crystallized and focused — where He is present with unusual power. They are sacramental moments: Scripture reading, the breaking of bread, baptism, reconciliation, anointing, gathering in prayer. Jesus appears not in victorious display but as an enabling sign to say, as He did to the two disciples at

Emmaus, "This is where I will be from now on." We meet the Risen and Transformed Christ in special liturgical moments and in special personal moments as well. He is a presence that is always with us, but at certain times we are able to experience not only the presence but the glory.

Point

One reason we experience the glory is so that we can say to others, "I have seen the Lord."

EASTER THURSDAY
Ac 3:11-26   *Lk 24:35-48*

First Reading

Both of today's readings are by the same author. His works are referred to as "Luke-Acts." In the Gospel reading the Lord tells His disciples to preach to the world beginning at Jerusalem. The Acts of the Apostles carries the story from Jerusalem to Rome. In today's first reading, we have Peter's speech in Jerusalem to his "fellow-Israelites." It is filled with Jewish imagery as can be seen from the titles given to Jesus: "Servant" (greatest of Old Testament titles), "Holy and Just One," "Author, Pioneer of New Life," "Messiah." All of these terms were loaded with Jewish history and meaning. They were also expressions of Jewish hopes and capture the Resurrection meaning from a Jewish point of view.

Gospel Reading

The Lord commissions the Apostles to carry the Gospel from Jerusalem to all the world. When these titles given to Jesus were taken to non-Jews, they had to be translated into words that could be comprehended. "Messiah" (Anointed) became "Christos" (Greek for Anointed) and almost a surname for Jesus. "Son of Man" became "Son of God"; "Servant" became "Word of God." The Church tried to express the reality of what the Risen Christ meant in terms which non-Jews could understand. Later councils and creeds would become increasingly metaphysical. That is one way in which the Gospel was preached to the ends of the earth and how it continues to be proclaimed. For ourselves, we might examine the meaning of the Resurrection for ourselves. How do we move from the fact that Jesus is no longer dead to its meaning as liberation from sin, healing, spiritual power and comforting presence? The Resurrection was the full display of God's glory and power. Different people tap into that victory and that glory in different ways. The power of God available to us through Jesus comes in many forms.

Point

The Resurrection can be a source of hope and power in every age, from Jerusalem to the ends of the earth.

EASTER FRIDAY
Ac 4:1-12   *Jn 21:1-14*

First Reading

One effect of the Resurrection was the eventual split of the Christian Church away from Judaism. In today's first reading, Peter and John stand before the Jewish high priests. In this scene, we are witnessing the start of the break with official

Judaism. It is the first skirmish and in later chapters the hostility will increase until Christianity will emerge as an independent entity. For the Apostles, who were Jewish Christians, the split was a very emotional event, like a separation from one's mother. For the Gentile Christians, such as Luke and the Church Fathers, it was more akin to a separation from one's mother-in-law. The final break was welcome for them. The Gospels must be read not only in the light of the Resurrection but also in the light of the antagonism the Church experienced from the Jewish leaders.

Gospel Reading

Judaism was conservative because it was built around the Torah Law. That Torah Law could be applied, interpreted and adapted but the psychological posture was that of preserving and keeping the Law. By contrast, Christianity thrust outward from the start. Unlike Judaism, it was intensely missionary. The disciples were sent to all nations (the probable reference of the 153 fish). The early Church had no hesitation in creating new offices, new rules, rearranging the Jewish liturgy to suit its own purposes and to speak in God's name. The reason for such energy and creativity was that at its center was not the Torah Law but the Holy Spirit of the Risen Lord Himself. The Christian Church has a dynamic center. At the center of our spiritual life is not an empty tomb or Torah Law but the Risen Lord Himself. His Spirit is present in our hearts urging us toward deeper faith and wider love.

Point

The spiritual vigor at the center of the Church derives not from a thing, but from a Person — the Risen Lord.

EASTER SATURDAY
Ac 4:13-21   Mk 16:9-15

First Reading

In this scene of Peter and John before the Jewish court, Luke is anxious to show that the early Church had not been engaged in anything illegal. It shows, as well, a gradual shift in leadership among the people from the official leaders of Judaism to the Christian Apostles. It highlights as well the new boldness with which the Apostles spoke. We can compare the hesitation, intramural quarreling and uncomprehending attitudes of these same men in Luke's Gospel. Pentecost had changed them. The same should be true of ourselves. We can draw spiritual confidence from the Spirit of the Risen Lord within us. People are often afraid to trust that Spirit. We should certainly read, consult and pray before important decisions of our life. Having done that, we should rely on the gift of the baptismal Spirit we have all received.

Gospel Reading

This ending of Mark's Gospel is interesting because it is one of several endings. This particular one is called canonical because it was pronounced inspired by the Council of Trent. Mark's original Gospel ends abruptly: the women see the empty tomb. Such an ending would be appropriate for the early Church. It would be similar to the story of the life of Cardinal Wojtyla ending with his arrival at the conclave. The rest of the story is well-known. Mark's original point was that we all fill in the story of the risen Christ in our own lives. Mark's Gospel had described what Jesus did during His public ministry as a prelude to what He continues to do through the Church. The story of the life of Jesus is meant to illustrate the ecclesial implications of the Risen power of Christ at work in the Church. What Jesus did back then, He continues to do now.

Point

We should never doubt the presence of the Risen Lord among us.

MONDAY — Second Week of Easter
Ac 4:23-31 *Jn 3:1-8*

First Reading

Today's first reading from the Acts of the Apostles contains an old prayer which some claim to be more ancient than the Passion accounts in the Gospels. It is a liturgical interpretation of the death of Christ. It beats with the realization that the persecution which these Christians are enduring is not simply random opposition but a parallel with the passion of Jesus. If Christians continue the ministry of the Lord, they are certain to continue His suffering. This is a powerful and comforting insight of Christian faith: if we look beneath the problems which we are enduring we will see the passion of Christ. Because of the Resurrection, our suffering now has the same redeeming power as did that of Jesus. Such an insight does not come easily.

Gospel Reading

Throughout the Gospel readings this week, we will consider the meeting of Nicodemus with Jesus. He was the man who came by night and represented the best of Judaism. He was a Pharisee, a Sanhedrin member and a rabbi. Some scholars say that since chronology is not that critical to John's

Gospel, it may well be that this interview occurred during Holy Week after the first meeting of the Sanhedrin. That would make this dialogue all the more powerful and haunting. Nevertheless, Nicodemus was attracted by Jesus' signs and teaching. The Lord wants to lead him to a deeper understanding of the kingdom. "Spirit" and "flesh" have specific meaning in a Johannine environment. The "flesh" sees only the surface of things. "Spirit" sees beneath appearances to the reality itself. This is one of the great themes of John's Gospel: to see through appearances and signs to the reality of the divine Lord. The Lord tells Nicodemus that such an insight is not an intellectual construct but the result of a complete change in the way a person lives. It is like being born all over again. Nicodemus responds that he is too old to change anymore. What is written is written. The Lord answers that this kind of birth is not a function of age. One can receive a new start in the spiritual life at any age.

Point

To see things as Jesus saw them, to see where the Spirit is and where He is not, is itself a gift of that Spirit.

TUESDAY — Second Week of Easter
Ac 4:32-37   Jn 3:7-15

First Reading

Today's first reading presents an ideal picture of the community life of the early Christians and the position of the Apostles. They shared things in common. Barnabas sold his farm and gave the proceeds to the Apostles. Ananias, skipped from today's reading, held back and was struck dead. This period of communal living did not last very long. Jerusalem was hit by a terrible famine and the community was in dire need. This was one reason for Paul's urgency in taking up the collection for the Jerusalem Church. Still, this picture remains an ideal for Christians in any era. It is not just a wistful ideal. Christians have tried and succeeded in living a community life in all kinds of ways, formal and informal. Further, this picture stems from the axial insight that to live out the Christian life requires not only community support but that this community embodies the presence of Christ among us. But we learn as well that the experience of community is very much a gift and does not appear by magic with the simple assemblage of a group of individuals.

Gospel Reading

This is the point of the Lord's words to Nicodemus. We are a community that believes God's love is revealed in suffering and death as well as in resurrection. Trying to create and sustain a community life has its own moments of suffering, death and resurrection. It is very easy to settle into our own private fantasy land of individual devotionalism. The presence of a community tests our faith and ties us to the real world. Just as the passion and death of Christ made His love for us concrete, so our effort to live with a community of faith stretches and deepens the reality of our faith.

Point

Community life is not easy but is vital. It is the testing ground for all we claim to be.

WEDNESDAY — Second Week of Easter
Ac 5:17-26   *Jn 3:16-21*

First Reading

In today's first reading, we see the central place which preaching held for the Apostles. They could easily have settled into being a private clique of believers and a secret society of sorts. But the public announcement of the good news was pivotal to everything they were. It raises the question for us as to what we see as central to our identity as Christians.

Gospel Reading

This Gospel reading is really a commentary on the Lord's dialogue with Nicodemus. Who practices evil in the darkness and who lives in the light is a searching question. We might examine the point at which those in the light start selling out to darkness. There does come a point when our light becomes dimmer. There are a number of instances where we proclaim the Risen Lord by action more than words. When a fellow Catholic goes through a divorce and then remarries in a Protestant church, our attendance might well make a statement. When children return home from college with a companion of the opposite sex, a parent's attitude toward their living together makes a statement. If we laugh at an off-color joke, we may well be making a statement. There are a number of ways in which we proclaim or fail to proclaim publicly our belief in the Risen Lord.

Point

We live by a light that shines in and outshines the darkness.

THURSDAY — Second Week of Easter
Ac 5:27-33   *Jn 3:31-36*

First Reading

This post-Pentecost scene in today's first reading reveals the new bravery in announcing the Gospel which Peter and the Apostles discovered. They are far different men from the fleeing and cowering disciples of Gethsemane. They have come to the light. More accurately, the Light poured in on them. They had received the Holy Spirit. The single sentence that capsulizes their new strength is the declaration that they must obey God rather than men.

Gospel Reading

This episode of Nicodemus' meeting with Jesus trails off without any clear conclusion. There is no rejection and no overwhelming acceptance of Christ. But a change does come over him. He appears two other times in John's Gospel. At the meeting of the Sanhedrin, he defends Jesus' due process right to a proper hearing. After the crucifixion, he appears with burial spices to bury Jesus like a king. So, perhaps, slowly he came to the light. At baptism, we receive the Holy Spirit. There is a certain romance to our image of the early Christians. We picture Victor Mature and Jane Russell running through the catacombs in one of many biblical movies. We imagine that if we were in their position we, too, would willingly suffer for our faith. But our temptations are more subtle. If because of our faith, we are faced with a loss of economic opportunity, cynical asides, the promotion of non-Christian values through the media, many of us do not remain very loyal to our relationship with Christ. Perhaps we start to retreat from the light toward darkness. We are in fact not generally faced with one great decision but a number of small decisions in which we either move closer to the light or farther from it.

Point

How much we risk for what we believe determines the depth with which we will experience eternal life.

FRIDAY — Second Week of Easter
Ac 5:34-42   *Jn 6:1-15*

First Reading

The Gamaliel of today's first reading was Paul's teacher. We sense storm clouds gathering. This is an important moment in the life of the Church. For the first five chapters of Acts, we have seen Peter and John preaching, healing a cripple, answering the Sanhedrin, escaping prison; the life lived in common; Barnabas' sale of his farm; Ananias' holding back. In all this, the Church was a Jewish Church. It was made up entirely of loyal Jews who attended the Temple and thought of Jesus as the fulfillment of Old Testament promises. Now, we are on the eve of the Church's transformation from a Jewish Church in Jerusalem into a worldwide, Gentile Church centered in Rome. The rest of Acts will deal with problems of universalism. The Apostles had fulfilled the command of the Lord. They preached the Gospel beginning in Jerusalem. They preached to their own before they moved outward.

Gospel Reading

John's recounting of the multiplication of the loaves is, as always, a symbol of the Eucharist. From these few loaves many were fed and made into a community, at least for a while. We are all faced with the problems of universalism in our own parishes and lives. We have to balance local needs with larger concerns. It would be scandalous to become so preoccupied with our own problems that we forget the larger world and its needs. The Apostles could have stayed in Jerusalem. Alternatively, we can become so preoccupied with other people's needs that we forget the serious problems we have within our own households. Everyone must strike a balance. The celebration of the Eucharist, symbolized in the Gospel, reminds us that there is in fact a balance to be struck between our personal world and the much larger world of mankind.

Point

The Eucharist reminds us that we are part of the larger Body of Christ.

SATURDAY — Second Week of Easter
Ac 6:1-7   Jn 6:16-21

First Reading

This first reading gives us a peek into the tensions of the early Church. We are told that the number of disciples grew. Packed into that brief sentence is a pivotal development that will occupy our attention for the next week. We are dealing here with two kinds of Jews. There were the Aramaic Jews, the Twelve, essentially conservative. They continued to frequent the Temple and saw themselves as Jews in every respect. There were also Greek-speaking Jews who did not speak Aramaic and were somewhat distanced psychologically, emotionally and theologically from Temple and Torah. They were much more liberal in their attitude toward traditional Jewish customs. In this first reading, the liberal group complains of inattention to their senior citizens. This caused the Twelve to create the office of deacon. The Greek names of the first deacons evidence the growth of this segment of the Church. This reading also illustrates the courage and ease with which the Twelve created new orders and institutions in the Church. They were confident that they acted in the Name of the Lord.

Gospel Reading

The sea was rough and the Lord appeared to the disciples. All of the storm sequences in the Gospels are recounted not only because of their miraculous resolution but also to indicate to the early Christians and to all future generations that the Lord is with the Church in any storm. In the growing distance between the Greek-speaking and the Aramaic-speaking Jewish Christians, the Lord will be present in that conflict not only to bring reconciliation through the Holy Spirit but to use that very tension as a spark that would propel the Gospel out of Jerusalem and into the wider, Gentile world. The Lord is with His people in any storm.

Point

Storms enable us to realize the Lord's presence and our need of each other.

MONDAY — Third Week of Easter
Ac 6:8-15   *Jn 6:22-29*

First Reading

With the forward stance of Stephen in today's first reading, we see the emergence of a germinal Church organization. The deacons were originally designated to wait on tables. Yet, very quickly, Stephen is preaching and engaging Jewish leaders in debate. He represents the Greek-speaking wing of the early Jewish Christian Church which was not as awed of Temple and Torah Law as were the more traditional Jewish Christians. The episode of Stephen's stoning signals a growing fracture between Church and Synagogue that was not inevitable but was providential. The Jewish leaders refused to go beneath the surface of things to examine more deeply what Stephen said.

Gospel Reading

In today's Gospel reading, we see the failure of the disciples to go beneath the surface of things to the deeper meaning of the miracle of the loaves. We all tend to react to appearances. We interpret the actions of others as hostility, aloofness or anger without probing more deeply into what these surface impressions might really be conveying. Paradoxically, we always find ways of justifying our own behavior. Throughout the Gospels, we see the Lord penetrating beneath the national, racial and sexual stereotypes of His time to what an individual is really saying, doing and feeling. To go beneath appearances is a skill and a gift of the Holy Spirit.

Point

If we knew each other as Jesus does, we would see how much we really are brothers and sisters in the Lord.

TUESDAY — Third Week of Easter
Ac 7:51-8:1 *Jn 6:30-35*

First Reading

Every generation reads history its own way. We can tell the decade in which a biblical movie was made by the very contemporary way in which supposedly ancient customs are portrayed. The same is the case with Stephen's speech which was omitted from the readings. He repeats the story of Abraham, Moses and David from a particular angle. This post-Resurrection speech saw the image of Jesus and His fate anticipated in the major figures of Jewish history. That discourse captures Stephen's attitude as well as that of Luke and the community for which he was writing. The essential difference is that Judaism saw the Temple and its ritual as the culmination of God's promise. It was the end product of Jewish history. Stephen and the Greek Jews saw it as an aberration. The great truths of "covenant" and "promise" were debased into a neurotic preoccupation with Temple precincts and rules. The result was a generation of spiritual death rather than life. The symbol failed to point. It became an end in itself.

Gospel Reading

Jesus not only gave new life to old symbols, such as the manna in the desert, but He gave a new covenant in which the Bread of Life would be available to every person. This entire intermediary system of Judaistic practices would be gone and the Lord would come to each individual directly as food. The result of Stephen's speech was not a personal triumph. He was stoned to death and it signalled the beginning of the break with the synagogue. But standing nearby was Saul. Stephen's message took root deep in Saul's heart. The themes of freedom from Law, Law as ministry of death, the letter of the Law as a killer while its spirit gives life would all reappear in his letters. The example we give, like that of Stephen, has a rebound effect. We also give fresh life to old symbols. People see the great truths of Christianity in a fresh way in our lives.

Point

Each of us is a fresh expression of the Gospel message.

WEDNESDAY — Third Week of Easter
Ac 8:1-8 *Jn 6:35-40*

First Reading

Today's first reading tells us that "a certain day" saw the beginning of a great persecution of the Church in Jerusalem. That day was the day Stephen was murdered or "executed." But who was persecuting whom? Evidently, the Twelve were safe. It was the Sanhedrin Jews who were persecuting the Greek-speaking Christian Jews. Our scene switches to Philip the deacon on his way to Samaria. The Samaritans were the half-breeds hated by the orthodox Jews of Jerusalem. Unlike Jerusalem which persecuted the Christians, the Samaritans are receptive to and enthusiastic about the Gospel. That persecution had the ironic effect of helping to spread the Gospel, in its Hellenistic version. The contrast between the sophisticated and unbelieving Jerusalem and the uncomplicated Samaritans reminds us that a simple, uncomplicated faith is what saves. Very often, a theoretical, academic approach to faith does not enhance our understanding but distances us from our original saving faith experience of the Lord.

Gospel Reading

The Lord asserts that He is the Bread of Life. We usually interpret that as referring to the Eucharist. It also means that Jesus is the Source of Life. He is the Staff of Life. Our relationship with Him should feed our theology, spirituality, poetry and song. Our knowledge of Jesus transfigures our world. Just as persecution provided the impetus for the evangelization of places to which the Jerusalem Christians might not otherwise have gone, so our knowledge of the Lord can transmute the problems of our life into spiritual energy.

Point

Our relationship with Christ is the molten core of everything Catholic about us.

THURSDAY — Third Week of Easter
Ac 8:26-40   Jn 6:44-51

First Reading

In today's first reading, we see the further movement of the Gospel from Jerusalem to Ethiopia in the person of the eunuch. Just as Jews wanted nothing to do with Samaritans, they wanted even less to do with eunuchs. This official is reading an Old Testament passage that becomes the basis for the deacon Philip's teaching and baptism. We have considered how people are drawn *to* the Lord. We might examine how they drift away from the Lord and from the Church. As in Philip's time, many today have never really heard the Gospel. There is a phenomenal religious illiteracy among people. This is one reason for the growth of a specific apostolate of evangelization — to bring the Gospel to people for the very first time. It has been said that of every hundred Catholics in the territory of a given parish, fifty will come to Church weekly, twenty-five will come regularly and the rest will not come at all. How then do people come back to the Lord and to the Church?

Gospel Reading

The Lord says that no one can come to Him unless the Father draws him. To each person God gives a sign. We see this recounted in so many conversion stories. For the eunuch it was an Old Testament passage. For Augustine, it was a child's singsong verse which he overheard. To each person, God gives something that captures and symbolizes what that individual is seeking. If that person responds, that is the beginning of faith. Studies have shown that of every five Catholics who have returned to the Church, three have done so because of an invitation by a fellow-Catholic to a religious or social function. Of course, we cannot force-feed the act of faith. We can set the stage and give an example while leaving room for the Holy Spirit to operate. What transpires deep inside a person's soul is between that individual and God.

Point

After we have done our best, the rest is up to the Holy Spirit.

FRIDAY — Third Week of Easter
Ac 9:1-20   *Jn 6:52-59*

First Reading

We can appreciate the hesitation of Ananias in meeting Paul. It would not be unlike Libya's Colonel Qadaffi appearing at a rectory door for convert instructions. One would have quite a few initial questions to ask him first. This conversion of Saul was a critical event in the Church's expansion. It is reported three times in the New Testament. The difficulty of reaching out to the Gentiles is shown from the fact that a miraculous intervention was required at each step forward. This event was also important for Paul. He who had persecuted the Church suddenly experienced faith, the Lord's love and freedom from the Torah Law all flooding in on him at once. And it was all free. This experience gave unity to his later life and theology. How did it change him? There would still be disagreements and bouts with his temper. It would take a while for this experience to sink in. The same is true for us. We have our religious experiences and afterwards our personal limitations do not completely disappear. It takes a while for our experience of the Lord to sink in. There are many little turnings in our life over a lifespan which is called to be an *en bloc* transformation in Christ. This gradual process gives unity to our life.

Gospel Reading

The Lord tells us why the Eucharist is important. "He who feeds on My flesh and drinks My blood has eternal life." We can use the analogy of food to make a spiritual point. We know what happens to those who eat in spurts. Those who starve themselves sooner or later will turn to any kind of junk food to assuage their hunger. The same is true of the spiritual life. Just as we need a steady and wholesome diet to grow physically, so we need a steady spiritual diet to grow in the Lord in a healthy way.

Point

Paul's conversion did not make him an instant saint. He was a saint only at the end of his life. The same is true of us. We become holy by gradual transformation.

SATURDAY — Third Week of Easter
Ac 9:31-42 *Jn 6:60-69*

First Reading

The mission to the Gentiles begins with Peter. Luke is using these incidents to track the spread of the Gospel northward from Jerusalem. Peter continues the ministry of Jesus. We are reminded through these healing that the power of the Lord was handed over to the Church. The very signs He worked are the identical works which the Apostles are empowered to do. More importantly, the identical spiritual ministry that Jesus performed during His earthly life of healing souls and forgiving sin was also entrusted to the Church. Although the physical healings are emphasized in Acts, the spiritual safety and renewal which the Church gives to people remain the heart of her mission and ministry.

Gospel Reading

The great eucharistic discourse in John's Gospel comes to an end. The reactions are mixed. Many disciples were dumbfounded; they could not see the point. They heard the words but missed the message. Jesus tells them that the faith He seeks is a gift for which one must be disposed. Many broke away because His message was not an obvious one of wonders and signs. Many left because He called for a conversion of life in order for a person to be enabled to see the import of what He was saying. The reaction of the Twelve is expressed by Peter who articulates an initial faith that will be deepened as time and events pass. He admits Jesus to be God's Holy One. That act of faith will begin Peter on a journey at the end of which he will be the cornerstone of apostolic faith and a martyr for the Lord.

Point

The gift of faith is not forced upon us. We must first be disposed to receive it.

MONDAY — Fourth Week of Easter
Ac 11:1-18   *Jn 10:1-10/10:11-18*

First Reading

The scene in today's first reading has been called the "Gentile Pentecost." We can again see how hard it was to break out of the Jewish mold and reach out to Gentiles. Up to this point, most of the people who were evangelized were half-Jews, semi-Jews, quasi-Jews, hemi-Jews, part-time Jews. Here, we have people who are completely non-Jews and were not interested in ever becoming Jews. Several points need notice. First, the surreal vision of Peter emphasized to him the non-binding character of the old dietary laws on Christians. He received that message through this powerful and unmistakable vision. Secondly, "those who were circumcised took issue with him." This indicates the position of Peter in this early community. The very fact that Peter ate with Gentiles indicates that the acceptance of the Gentiles on non-Jewish terms was no position of a lunatic fringe. It was a position that deserved serious consideration. Thirdly and most important, they received the Holy Spirit and were then baptized. Peter gives sacramental recognition to what was actually going on. It was a recognition that ritual cannot be divorced from reality. In all of this, we see the Church following the Lord and not the Lord following the Church.

Gospel Reading

The Lord calls Himself the Good Shepherd. There are others who do not yet belong to this fold. The Lord was indicating that there were more members to His flock than the disciples, than the Jews and, to us, than the Roman Catholics. This reading keeps us humble. It reminds us that what we do as a Church does not exhaust the activity and reach of the Risen Lord. Jesus works and moves through His Spirit outside the boundaries of Church Law and structure. That is His way of leading us to areas where we would not otherwise go. By expanding the Church's apostolate in unconventional directions, we are recognizing reality — that the Spirit of God acts beyond the limits of the Church. Our mission as a Church is to focus, concentrate, project and effect what is implicitly the case in the world of the Spirit. We give a name to the God who moves so many people.

Point

We find the presence of Jesus in unexpected places. We cannot program the Lord. The Church follows Him.

TUESDAY — Fourth Week of Easter
Ac 11:19-26   *Jn 10:22-30*

First Reading

Antioch was one of the three greatest cities of the Mediterranean along with Alexandria and Rome. Here, the Gospel was brought to uncircumcised pagans in a formal way. They were converted. The Jerusalem Church sent Barnabas to incorporate

them into the fold and "give them envelopes." Note the sequence. They talk with the Christians and are converted. Then
teachers are sent to articulate the content of what they have
come to believe. That sequence is vital because seldom does
teaching initiate faith. At Antioch, the name "Christian" was
used for the first time. This means that in this cosmopolitan
center, pagans could now tell the difference between this
group of believers, Judaism and pagan cults. We are witnessing
in these weeks of Easter the growing self-awareness of the
Church. Precisely under the pressure of events, the real foundation of the Church is laid bare as not resting on Moses, Torah
Law or Temple but on Jesus Christ. He was the new foundation
of faith. The faith of the Church was becoming clarified through
experience.

Gospel Reading

The Lord declares Himself and the Father to be One. As
time went on, this statement of the Lord would be clarified. Are
Jesus and the Father one thing? Are they two phases of one
thing? Do they think alike? Will alike? Love alike? Thus are
doctrines born. We go through the same process. Our faith is
clarified and matured through experience. We all have good
times and bad. The point is not to insulate our faith from them. It
is important that our believing grow together with our experiencing. Then, not only will events that occur in our life help
us explore the implications of our faith but our faith will help us
experience them in the light of the Lord.

Point

*Like the early Church, our believing should grow with our
experiencing.*

WEDNESDAY — Fourth Week of Easter
Ac 12:24-13:5   *Jn 12:44-50*

First Reading

It all looks so easy in today's first reading. They were
engaged in the liturgy and the Holy Spirit speaks. Is that how it
happens? Let us look at some points in today's first reading.
Barnabas and Saul (note the order of the names) returned *from*
Jerusalem after their relief mission. Antioch was evidently run
by prophets and teachers (which means trouble). There was a
great desire to bring the Gospel to the ends of the earth. On that
they were all agreed. The question of what would be required
of the Gentiles upon admission caused difficulties. We all want
a meaningful liturgy, dynamic parish and community spirit.
Trying to see how that might be achieved uncovers a variety of
methods. The early Church had no easy answers. There was the
give and take of discussion, persuading, politicking — and in
all that the Holy Spirit was at work. This final supervening
element of the Spirit is what Luke emphasizes. In today's first
reading, we have the final moment of agreement. Yes! The
Holy Spirit wants Barnabas and Saul. That event was the result
of a long process.

Gospel Reading

There are several important principles to remember when
we wonder how the Holy Spirit speaks to us. First, Jesus' words
are God's word to us. "Whoever looks on Me has seen the
Father." Secondly, in prayer, we come to understand that
word. Its implications and meaning do not automatically fly off
the page to us. Thirdly, we should look for confirmation of that
word to us in other places and events of our life. Fourthly, we
should engage in Christian conversation about it with our

fellow-Christians. Finally, we should look into our past to see
the direction in which the Lord is leading us. Luke telescopes a
long process. Throughout that long process, the Holy Spirit is at
work.

Point

*The Holy Spirit does not have a gospel of His own. He
enables us to understand and apply the words of the Lord Jesus
to ourselves.*

THURSDAY — Fourth Week of Easter
Ac 13:13-25   Jn 13:16-20

First Reading

Today's first reading speaks about Paul and his companions (note the new order of the names). Antioch in Pisidia
(Turkey) was named after a great Greek general named Anti-
ochus. We have two cases of double-cross in today's readings.
It is something we all have experienced. The first reading
indicates that John Mark left them and returned to Jerusalem.
We do not know the reason but Paul found it hard to forgive (Ac
15:36-41). Mark then disappears for a while until Paul is in
prison. He wrote to Timothy, "Get Mark and bring him with
you for he is very helpful to me." This deserter became a
Gospel writer and the person Paul wanted at his side in his last
days.

Gospel Reading

In this reading, we have the Last Supper scene. Jesus
washed the feet of His Apostles as a symbol and example. With

Judas among them, He said they would be blessed if they did the same for each other as He had done. Later He quotes Psalm 41, "Even the one I trusted, who ate bread with me has lifted his heel against me." Reconciliation was still possible, but Judas went his own way. Reconciliation was refused. Judas created his own punishment.

We have two cases: reconciliation refused and reconciliation achieved. What is distinctive about the Christian community and ourselves as Christians is not that we have conflict. The only way to avoid conflict is to put an entire parish on Valium. What is important is that we reconcile with each other. This is what should distinguish us from others. Like Paul and Mark, we should be able to forgive and, unlike Judas, be willing to accept forgiveness.

Point

Forgiving and being forgiven are the stuff of Christian growth.

FRIDAY — Fourth Week of Easter
Ac 13:26-33 *Jn 14:1-6*

First Reading

Paul recounts the story of the Jewish people up to David and then skips to Jesus and the events of the Passion. This sermon was probably typical of the kind of missionary sermon that was given to Jewish communities around the known world. Paul shows how all of salvation history converges and pours into Jesus. He also adds a tiny polemic against the obduracy of the officials at Jerusalem. The sermon is much larger than what is contained in our readings. After rehearsing this history, Paul's point is that full and final forgiveness of all sin is now available for free in Jesus. Sins of which even the Mosaic Law could not acquit anyone can now be forgiven through belief in Jesus. The leaders ask Paul to return again to speak. We should note that Paul made the subject of repentance and reconciliation comprehensible to the Jews through speaking in terms of their own history. In this sense, it is a model sermon for evangelizers. We apply its lesson by showing people today the totality of the redeeming act of Jesus in psychological, social and personal terms.

Gospel Reading

The Lord speaks before the Ascension. He tells His disciples that He must go away. Thomas was puzzled as to the exact destination of the Lord. Jesus answers him not with heavenly directions or ancient cosmology but with the assurance that He is the way, truth and life. The Lord says that to know what and where heaven is, we should remain in Him. We will then have some experience of the glory, the deep healing, the joy and fulfillment which heaven is. Our access to the domain of God is only through Jesus. What that fulfillment of heaven is will depend on our needs, wounds and searchings. Generically, it is fulfillment. The concrete shape of that fulfillment depends on our needs and psychological framework.

Point

The objective truths of our religion must be preached in a way that satisfies the human needs they were meant to address.

SATURDAY — Fourth Week of Easter
Ac 13:44-52   Jn 14:7-14

First Reading

In today's first reading, we see the preaching of the Gospel move forward with unstoppable power. The whole town gathered to hear Paul. The jealousy of the Jews foments a mini-rebellion against Paul which gets him expelled from the town. This is decisive because Paul now decides to spend his efforts preaching directly to and for Gentiles. This tiny persecution that the Jews had drummed up became, once again, the engine for the further dissemination of the Gospel to Iconium in Galatia. The experiences Paul had with Jewish leaders were slowly reinforcing the theological conclusions about the Law to which he had already come on other grounds.

Gospel Reading

Philip asks to see the Father. The import of his question is to have the Lord finally show them the glory, power and majesty of the Father. Jesus' reply is simple and arresting. Those who have seen Him have seen the Father. We cannot look at the face of God for God is Spirit. But we can see the face of Jesus as He is portrayed in the Gospels. He shows us all we need to know of God. Jesus is the living revelation. Further, the Lord's assertion says something about the Church as well. We hear grand descriptions of the role of the Church and its place as an agent of reconciliation. To find this exalted Church, we have only to look at the faces of people in our parish. This is the community Jesus founded and which He loves. To people such as us have been entrusted His word, His power of reconciliation and His love for mankind. It is a great dignity and a great challenge.

Point

The power of God shines out of human eyes.

MONDAY — Fifth Week of Easter
Ac 14:5-18   *Jn 14:21-26*

First Reading

Paul and Barnabas arrive at a pagan town. This is the first sermon in the New Testament addressed directly to non-Jews. Paul refers not to the Scriptures or to sacred history but to nature and human experience for clues as to the nature of God. Paul moved from things people knew to what they did not yet know. The same process occurs today in different ways. Without revelation, prophecies or the Lord Jesus, what would we know about God? We all have an instinct for God. We would turn to nature to fill out our picture of God. We would look to physical nature and to human nature. Sometimes the resulting image of God took grotesque forms but there is a universal sense of something beyond the world we see. That awareness is present in our technocratic and secular culture. Even though many try to suppress that God instinct, it manifests itself in popular interest in superstition, the preternatural, cults or the adulation of celebrity (as happened to Paul in today's first reading). All of this manifests our built-in instinct for God. In the Old Testament, we have a record of an increasingly clear perception of God together with God's progressive revelation of Himself to us. The culmination of that process was Jesus Christ.

Gospel Reading

The Lord turns the attention of the disciples from curiosity about His final manifestation at the end of time to an important revelation of Himself to believers who must live in the interim before the age comes to a close. This is the abiding presence of Jesus in our hearts through His Spirit. This is an intimate and personal presence of Christ that is more vivid and convincing than merely intellectual demonstrations of His identity. It is the apex of the human search for God. This is the presence that issues not in more ideas primarily but in love.

Point

The State, money or celebrity can be deified. The ways to God are many. The most personal and abiding is to discover the Lord within.

TUESDAY — Fifth Week of Easter
Ac 14:19-28 *Jn 14:27-31*

First Reading

Antioch seems to have been the home base from which the missionary journeys to the Gentiles were sent out. This first reading gives some partial evidence of the persecutions and Jewish posses that followed Paul and his disciples. It also exhibits the tremendous devotion Paul must have inspired among his companions. In each community, he established some germinal structure and then returned to the home base at Antioch to report all that had happened. His trials show the difficulty that attended the spread of the Gospel. Local Jews often managed to arrange a hostile welcome party to ward Paul off. Each time a mini-persecution takes place, it has the effect of moving the Gospel forward. It served to strengthen the resolve of Paul, his companions and newly created disciples.

Gospel Reading

The Lord describes the peace He gives to those who follow Him. That peace was a permanent gift to His disciples. It is not a secular peace. It does not mean the absence of hostility from others or lack of tension in our own ranks. The peace of the Lord is peace at our center. It derives from our knowing we are reconciled with the Father and safe in His care. The hostility of others cannot disturb this peace. It is an assurance that God is on our side. It is strengthened by the basic agreement we have with others on the Lordship of Jesus in our lives. It is only those who know they are in such profound agreement who can allow disagreement over method to exist. Only those who are unsure about agreement in basics are concerned about the slightest discordance. Their unity is so fragile that any disagreement can break it apart. The peace of the Lord is deep, primal and healing.

Point

Peace at the center enables us to endure any unrest and opposition from the outside.

WEDNESDAY — Fifth Week of Easter
Ac 15:1-6   Jn 15:1-8

First Reading

We have the early warning signs of the first great controversy which will rock the early Church. It is the issue of circumcision. It will consume a great part of many of Paul's letters. It will be the occasion for the final showdown between the Jewish Christians and the Gentile Christians. Some of the Jewish Christians saw the Church as simply a segment — a special, holy, saving segment — of Judaism. Christianity was the nucleus for the revival of Judaism. Accordingly, all the Jewish practices and rituals were to be binding on all new Christians. For Barnabas and Paul, seasoned now by several missionary visits among Gentiles, this was dead wrong. Christianity's future lay as a new covenant away from the old rituals of Judaism. Christianity was a new Israel. The Apostles decided to convene a meeting which would become known in history as the Council of Jerusalem. The theological issue is whether there is any saving power left in the old rituals. The political issue was the identity of the Christian movement. Out of all this, Christianity will emerge as a Gentile Church.

Gospel Reading

The Lord states that He is the real vine. The vine was an Old Testament image for Israel. In effect, the Lord declares Himself to be the real Israel. The image of vine and branches enables us to consider the subject of dead wood. It is as applicable to today's first reading as to our own spiritual life. First, the early Church was not simply an offshoot or branch of Judaism. This will be the outcome of the great debate. It will settle for all time that the Church is grafted onto the Lord Jesus and not onto the old covenant. We can apply that image to our spiritual life. A branch that is cut off from the main stock continues to look healthy but, in fact, it is dead. It has been disconnected from the source of life. The same can happen when we cut ourselves off from the Lord. We can continue to go through the motions and look like functioning Christians. But we are living off fumes. We are simply going through the motions. Our prayer becomes boring, liturgical services carry no lift, there is nothing to praise about the Church, our time with the community of faith becomes non-existent. We are dead. The sacraments remain our lifeline to the Lord.

Point

The source of spiritual vitality is the Lord. Nothing can replace Him as the source of spiritual life or eternal life.

THURSDAY — Fifth Week of Easter
Ac 15:7-21   Jn 15:9-11

First Reading

The Council of Jerusalem is going with full force. Peter speaks of his own experience of preaching to the Gentiles and the sudden gift of the Spirit he had witnessed them receive. Discussion continued no longer. Finally, James, elder of the Jerusalem Church, stood to give his appeal for a compromise position that would not offend the conservative Jewish Christian wing nor burden the Gentile converts. The few practices they required were those well-known as binding upon strangers living in Israel. Since the Law had been read throughout the known world, James reasons that the Gentiles would have no difficulty abiding by these familiar regulations. This solution seems to have brought some measure of repose to the issue. Paul's account of this meeting in the second chapter of Galatians is a case study in selective perception.

Gospel Reading

The Lord speaks about His own commandments. The reference is not directly to the Ten Commandments but to love of God and of neighbor as well as to other admonitions we find throughout the Gospels. The Lord is not inviting a new Christian itemization as much as He is calling us to a way of life, a way of experiencing God. It would be unfortunate to delimit this new way of life to a series of precise practices that would be seen as exhausting the Christian vocation. The love of God can be expressed in many ways as can love of neighbor. The thrust of the Gospel is actually to appreciate the dynamic contained in the gift of the Spirit and to leave our ways of deepening love to be open-ended.

Point

The full experience of the Christian life requires that we transcend a specific set of requirements into viewing the Christian discipleship as a way of living all of our life.

FRIDAY — Fifth Week of Easter
Ac 15:22-31   *Jn 15:12-17*

First Reading

The compromise was crafted. The letter stated the minimal requirements expected of Gentile entrants into the Christian community by the Jerusalem Church. These requirements seem to have disappeared over time. There is a relativity to Church rules. The instructions contained in this first reading are very time-bound. They were written to preserve the sensitivities of Jewish Christians in this first generation of the Church. As these Jewish Christians died, the rationale for these rules would cease to exist. The same is true of many regulations enjoined upon Church members whose contents are not doctrinal but are designed to preserve the sensitivities of a minority or majority. This issue is not a first-century relic. The adaptation of

Christianity today in Africa and Asia raises identical issues of the line between the doctrinal and the cultural.

Gospel Reading

Some have said that these words of the Lord are John's version of the missionary discourse found in different form in the Synoptic Gospels. The Lord's command that we love each other takes shape in ways that are culturally bound. The generic, overriding command is incumbent on all Christians. How we express that love in societies that are socialist, capitalist, urban or agricultural will differ. There is a critical distinction between principle and practice. There are lots of ways of loving and of not loving. Jesus is the universal model of how to love. He showed love in a variety of ways during His ministry. Our small efforts to love combine to make a powerful current of God's love that flows from God through us to others. It is our missionary work.

Point

Rules give cultural expression to an unalterable divine command to love one another.

SATURDAY — Fifth Week of Easter
Ac 16:1-10   *Jn 15:18-21*

First Reading

The Council of Jerusalem is over and Paul continues his missionary work among the Gentiles. He took as a companion Timothy, a man considered illegitimate by Jewish law. Paul had him circumcised to gain credibility among the Jews. In this reading, we see how Luke interjects himself into the account in one of several "we" sections. The impulse of the Lord to Paul to continue his missionary work comes through dreams, invitations, decisions and persecutions. The Holy Spirit is at work in all this, propelling Paul and the Gospel forward.

Gospel Reading

Jesus closely identifies the Church's fortunes with His own life. The Church must expect persecutions and harassment because the same happened to the Lord. This is a reminder that the pain He endured was not simply an historical accident. It was part of God's plan that the preaching and living of the Word would always put one at odds with the world. The fact that a person represents light makes those in darkness want to extinguish him or her. The Lord makes these statements not only to encourage His disciples but also as words for them to recall during times of harassment. The fact of their persecution will be an authentic piece of evidence that they are faithful to the Lord's mission. It is only when the Church becomes cozy with society and attains a privileged position with various governments that we have an indicator that something may be profoundly wrong.

Point

Popular opposition is one sign that the Church is doing something exactly right.

MONDAY — Sixth Week of Easter
Ac 16:11-15   Jn 15:26-16:4

First Reading

In today's first reading, Paul goes to Philippi, a kind of retirement community and tax haven for wealthy Romans. This is Paul's entry into Europe. There, he met Lydia, a dealer in "purple goods." She was a wealthy and independent business-woman who provided a nucleus of people and a base of operations for Paul. He always wrote with affection about the Philippian Christians. We all need a home base and place to recharge. We need a place where we can regroup and draw new strength from others. This is especially true in the spiritual domain. We need a spiritual home, a place and people where, like Paul, we can become reinvigorated.

Gospel Reading

The Lord describes the traumatic experiences ahead for the Christians. They would be "expelled from the synagogue." This event would be devastating for the traditional Jewish Christians because the synagogue was their spiritual home. It was not such for the Antiochene Christians. This was one reason why the celebration of the Eucharist became so vital and valuable. It became what the synagogue had been and a great deal more as well. The obligation to celebrate the Eucharist is not our way of doing a favor for God. It is for ourselves. We need a place to recharge, a place of faith, a place of Christian memory and of Christian hope. This is what our Eucharist is. It is the place, as the Lord indicates in today's Gospel reading, where the Spirit bears witness, convinces us again and brings new life to our faith.

Point

The eucharistic celebration is our spiritual home, wherever we may travel.

TUESDAY — Sixth Week of Easter
Ac 16:22-34   *Jn 16:5-11*

First Reading

In this first reading, Paul and Silas are in jail. There had been a possessed girl in Philippi who was employed as a fortune teller. Paul cured her and put her employer out of work. He then incited a mob against Paul and Silas. They were arrested. He was not. Here, the jailer finds himself in the center of a personal crisis. The release of Paul and Silas made him look incompetent. That crisis made him look for a deeper source of salvation. It is often the case that national, international or personal crisis can turn us to things of the Spirit. The structures we build and upon which we rely show themselves, at different points, to be fragile. Not unimportant, but fragile. We all build little routines and procedures to introduce some predictability into our world. We all have a morning routine; take the same seat in church; read the newspaper in the same order. We tend to endow these things with greater reliability than they deserve. Then, our friends prove untrue, we lose a job, an earthquake shakes our home, we have a brush with death and we realize how vulnerable we really are. It was the fall of almighty Rome that caused Saint Augustine to look for real security in the City of God. The dismantling of the jailer's future triggered faith.

Gospel Reading

We have a language problem in today's Gospel reading. "Paraclete" means Advocate, Lawyer, Attorney. The Lord says that He will prove the world wrong about quite a few things. The heavenly Lawyer will show the world what sin really is — refusal to believe in the Lord. He will enable them to realize that justice is tempered by God's mercy available now because Jesus has gone to the Father. He will help them realize that there is deliverance from condemnation because of the power of the Resurrection. When we are faced with a crisis that breaks apart the fragile security that we have, that fissure in our life allows the Holy Spirit to enter to change our notions of religion, God, faith and life. It can transform the way we see the world. Then the process of conversion and renewal begins.

Point

The Holy Spirit enters in the cracks of our lives to enable us to see where real security and abiding strength are. That Spirit strengthens the part of us that will never die — our relationship with Christ.

WEDNESDAY — Sixth Week of Easter
Ac 17:15, 22-18:1   Jn 16:12-15

First Reading

In today's first reading, a man called Dionysius of the court of Areopagus is mentioned. His name comes down in history as Dionysius the Areopagite. An interesting story attaches to him. Around the year 600, a book was written about angels called the *Celestial Hierarchy*. It was a detailed account about everything anyone ever wanted to know about angels but was afraid to ask. To insure its credibility, the name of Dionysius was appended as the author. That carried the work into the Middle Ages as authoritative and it was relied upon by the great medieval thinkers. That author has become known as Pseudo-Dionysius. In Athens, there was no Athenian Church. Paul did not establish one. They turned away at the message of the Resurrection. When Paul spoke about more than general principles of religion and became particular, they walked away. They heard the Gospel as something to be analyzed but not to be embraced. The convincing power of the Spirit did not reach them.

Gospel Reading

The Lord describes the functions of the Paraclete, or Holy Lawyer. He will tell us what to say and how to say it. The Paraclete works not only when Christians are called before investigating committees but also when we face aperson's personal crisis. The Holy Spirit enables us to say the right thing. Secondly, that Spirit will guide us into truth. It is from the Spirit that our right and bright ideas come. Thirdly, that Spirit will guide us to action. In complex situations, we will be guided by the Holy Spirit almost instinctively. All of this is a function of how deeply we allow the Spirit to permeate our lives. The Holy Spirit does not come only for ecumenical councils and confirmations. He is an abiding, permanent source of life, renewal and inspiration that we cannot lose. We can tune that Spirit out, but cannot lose Him.

Point

If the new life of the Spirit is not put into action, the old way of life will reclaim our consciousness.

THURSDAY — Sixth Week of Easter
Ac 18:1-8   *Jn 16:16-20*

First Reading

One of the constants of Paul's apostolate to the Gentiles is his repeated encounters with Jewish Christians as well as random groupings of Christians scattered throughout the regions he enters. Paul's great achievement was his assembling these individuals into small, coherent seed communities. Those communities may have been composed of relatively few people but they were the base from which he could move into the larger Gentile world. They became a magnet which attracted others interested in hearing and living the Gospel. Paul's communities were administrative marvels. His letters give some evidence that problems with them abounded. But they were communities with an identity and a definite view of the redeeming work of Christ that had been learned from Paul. This set of communities became the seedbed that endured long after Paul was gone and provided the source of Christian influence throughout the region. Although we know of Paul's activities in the major centers whose letters have been preserved, we know only indirectly of the effect, for example, of the Corinthian Christians on the larger community of Corinth. The full story remains hidden with the Lord. But they did have an effect.

Gospel Reading

The return of Jesus to the Father meant that He would no longer be visibly present among His disciples. In His stead, He would send His Spirit to permeate the community and continue His ministry. If Jesus had remained among His disciples as a visible and risen presence, they would naturally submerge their initiative and individuality to Him. He wanted the community He created and nourished to be filled with His Spirit so they could transmit the message to others. This is one reason for the Ascension and the sending of the Spirit. The entire history of salvation culminates not in the Resurrection of the Lord but in the flooding of the Spirit into people's minds and hearts to fulfill the vision of the prophet Joel.

Point

The purpose of the death and Resurrection of Christ was to send the Spirit into the hearts of people.

FRIDAY — Sixth Week of Easter
Ac 18:9-18   *Jn 16:20-23*

First Reading

The theme of today's readings is the promise and the pain involved in giving birth to the kingdom. In our first reading, we see Paul in Corinth accused by the Jews. Gallio, the government official, viewed this as an intramural religious debate and refused to become involved. He dismisses the case. Then Sosthenes, who had whipped the people into a frenzy against Paul, had the frenzy turn on him. Paul's mission to Corinth turned out to be successful. In First Corinthians, he refers to "Sosthenes, our brother."

Gospel Reading

The Lord describes the pain of giving birth to the Gospel. The oscillation of low and high points in Paul's ministry was like giving birth. We have the promise of the kingdom in our lives and in our world. But, it is difficult to maintain enthusiasm. Building the kingdom is not like building a castle. We are dealing with human beings, free will and grace. Now and then, we receive consolations (as the medievals called them) or moments of grace when we experience some preliminary results of our work. There are times when we glimpse the Lord's presence and see the purpose of our labor. That gives us new strength to continue and to continue to continue. Only at the end, will we see how everything fits together. Then our questions will be answered. Then we will understand the pain and the promise.

Point

We cannot avoid the pain. But we should never forget the Lord's promise.

SATURDAY — Sixth Week of Easter
Ac 18:23-28   *Jn 16:23-28*

First Reading

We meet Apollos in today's first reading. He was a very effective teacher who could speak persuasively about the Messianic fulfillment of the Jewish prophets found in Jesus. This is the Apollos toward whom Paul was very ambivalent because of the divisions that occurred in the Corinthian Church after his departure. The reading is puzzling because it is difficult to discern Apollos' theological point of departure. He speaks persuasively about Jesus but seems to know only of John's baptism of Jesus. His knowledge of the Gospel was only partial. For that, he needed further instruction from Priscilla and Aquila. After this reality-testing of his own conclusions with the apostolic teaching, he was set to go on another preaching tour of the region. There is no reason to subscribe to the popular caricature of him as an intentionally divisive figure. He was one of the great evangelizers of the New Testament. What he lacked was the fullness of the Gospel that came from knowledge of the pouring of the Spirit in baptism that can infuse people's beings. In other words, salvation was more than something Jesus achieved on the Jordan. It was something He shared at Pentecost.

Gospel Reading

The Lord speaks about a time when He will no longer use veiled language in speaking of the Father. Then, our joy will be full. Jesus refers to the Pentecost event for the Apostolic college and to baptism for our individual selves. When we receive the Holy Spirit, we are no longer dependent on words, images or phrases of a teacher to instruct us about something of which we know little. We are able to experience the presence of God for ourselves. It is similar to the experience of love. One can hear lectures and read books about love. It is only when an individual has the experience of love that she or he can realize the full depth of its power as something much more than words can convey. The same is true of our experience of God. Once we experience the Spirit's presence in our hearts, then we realize the partiality of all language and theologies of the Spirit.

Point

The Spirit enables us to experience what we have heard being taught and preached.

MONDAY — Seventh Week of Easter
Ac 19:1-8   *Jn 16:29-33*

First Reading

In today's first reading, Paul is in Ephesus. Ephesus was something of a commercial center, the Hong Kong of the Mediterranean. He stayed there longer than anywhere else.

The people he met were incomplete Christians. They knew only the baptism of John (thanks to Apollos). The difference between the preaching of John and that of the Lord is that John spoke of threats to make people aware of sin. He spoke of condemnation to generate an effort to repent. The Lord spoke of forgiveness. Through the mercy of Jesus, condemnation was taken away. We are speaking here of two stages in the growth of a mature faith. Many people know the religion of struggle but not of peace. They know of condemnation and the effort to repent but do not know of the grace and love of Christ or of the gift of the Holy Spirit. We can, of course, lose a sense of sin by making sin too trivial or too private an affair. Catholic theology seeks to engender a healthy, accurate sense of sin while speaking of forgiveness and the regenerating power of the Holy Spirit.

Gospel Reading

In today's Gospel reading, the disciples claim to believe. The Lord states that the experience of sin will come into their lives when they flee and abandon Him. Only when they return will they find peace and forgiveness. The point of our Christian faith is not to become preoccupied with the presence of sin. After we receive our *mea culpas*, it is critical that we take the next step to find peace and inner harmony.

Point

Repentance does not look to the past. It looks to the future.

TUESDAY — Seventh Week of Easter
Ac 20:17-27   *Jn 17:1-11*

First Reading

Both of today's readings read like the finale of a play, the concluding argument to a jury. Both Paul and Jesus look back over a life and a ministry. In today's first reading, Paul is on his way to Jerusalem which will be, for him, the beginning of the end. He realizes that and has no regrets. His life fulfilled the mission given him by the Lord. All the events and opportunities given him were used to the full.

Gospel Reading

In this Gospel reading, one of the most intimate sections of John's Gospel, we have the prayer of Jesus as He looks back over His own ministry. He also used all the opportunities the Father had given Him. Paul stated that he had not shrunk from announcing God's design. The Lord says that He has made the Father's name known.

It can happen that we miss the opportunities the Lord gives us by always living in the future. "Tomorrow, I will get down to my spiritual life." "Tomorrow, I will start spending more time with my family." "Tomorrow, we'll reconcile." Or, we can live in the past as we refight old battles and rehearse old hurts. It is in the present that the dynamics of salvation take place. God's word is spoken to us in the now. Christ's offer of peace and the healing power of the Resurrection are available to us now. The time of salvation and of the experience of God's presence are now. It is in this particular parish, this neighborhood, with these people, that God is present and calling.

Point

We can miss God's call to us by concentrating on the future or on the past. God is with us in the now.

WEDNESDAY — Seventh Week of Easter
Ac 20:28-38   *Jn 17:11-19*

First Reading

In today's first reading, Paul is on his way to Jerusalem as the end of his ministry begins. He charges the leaders of the Church at Ephesus to keep watch for wolves who would lead the flock astray. We might consider what causes corrosion in the Church both on the universal and local levels. Theological error is part of it. Studies have shown, however, that people drop out of the Church for a number of reasons: mobility without deep religious roots, too little or too much change, deterioration of Catholic family life, diminishing loyalty to a specific parish, impersonalism of the large parish, a quarrel with or perceived insult from a priest or nun. The major reasons that people drop out of the Church are more personal than they are theological.

Gospel Reading

Jesus asks the Father to guard the flock from the evil one. The Lord is not simply speaking of theological error. He refers to the way of the world. We are all Christ's Body in the world. What people see, hear and touch of Christ is us. For better or worse, we are the Body of Christ not to Russia, China or Chile but to the people around us. It is through people that faith is strengthened or weakened. We are the carriers of the living Christ. This is one reason why Paul is so insistent about the personnel who will find their way into the Ephesian Church and why the Lord prays that the evil one will be warded off. It is those who can infect a community with suspicion and quarreling that can destroy a community's sense of the Lord's presence and His mission for them.

Point

A community is weakened or strengthened not by theories but by people.

THURSDAY — Seventh Week of Easter
Ac 22:30;23:6-11   *Jn 17:20-26*

First Reading

The Sadducees were a priestly and aristocratic class. They were the "high priest's party" about which we read in the Gospels. They wanted the Law observed exactly as written without interpretation. They were representative of the "old time religion" without any modern additions or dilutions. The Pharisees, on the other hand, were a lay movement. There were about 6000 of them. They were the liberals of their day. For them, the observance of the Torah Law together with their interpretation of it was important. Although the bulk of the Law was from the past, subsequent interpretations became as important as the Law itself. They tried to make the Law livable in a changing environment. The Lord's criticism of them was that these interpretations became as sacred as the Law itself. In today's first reading, Paul exploits the animosity between these two groups to his own advantage. The Pharisees survived the destruction of the Temple and are the ancestors of orthodox Judaism today.

Gospel Reading

The Lord speaks about His gift of peace to us and to the Church. In our own day, we have experienced divisions similar to those that split Pharisees and Sadducees. Such sharp divisions are never entirely healthy. They drain energy, time and intellectual effort from more productive enterprises. It can happen that because of such divisions, a Roman Catholic will be more hospitable to a Buddhist than to a fellow Catholic. The maintenance of unity in diversity is a difficult question. We can preserve unity in prayer by keeping our focus on the Lord. There are so many forces that pull apart families, parishes and people. Unity, cohesion and fidelity as a Church are indeed gifts of the Spirit. The Lord has not given us an idea to hold us together. He has given us the force and power of the Holy Spirit.

Point

Unity is a gift from the Lord.

FRIDAY — Seventh Week of Easter
Ac 25:13-21   Jn 21:15-19

First Reading

Throughout this whole trip back to Jerusalem, we do not get the impression that Paul is entirely a victim of circumstances. He is very capable of manipulating the system to his own advantage. Yesterday, we saw his exploitation of the strong animus between Pharisees and Sadducees. Now, in today's first reading, he appeals to the emperor. As a result, he will receive a trip to Rome at government expense — a place to which he wanted to go in the first place. He preached in Rome for two years. It was a time of great courage and faith for Paul.

Gospel Reading

Peter provides a contrast with Paul. He had denied the

Lord and, in today's Gospel reading, we witness the Lord forgiving him. In this scene, Jesus drew out courage, leadership and faith from Peter that otherwise might well have been smothered in a morass of self-denial and self-recrimination. Peter and Paul both exhibit the effect of the Holy Spirit upon us. The Holy Spirit will not turn a poet into an economist. But the Spirit enables us to center, control and clarify the gifts we have so that we can live as God intended. The effect of the Spirit on Peter and Paul was to strengthen their natural abilities. The Spirit redirected Paul's fire. The Spirit channeled Peter's leadership and stability. The Spirit helps us mold, shape and transform our gifts into instruments of the Lord.

Point

The Spirit helps us to see things more clearly, to love God more dearly and to follow Christ more nearly.

SATURDAY — Seventh Week of Easter
Ac 28:16-20, 30-31   *Jn 21:20-25*

First Reading

This is our final scene of Paul. He is lodged in Rome, waiting for a hearing and continuing to preach the Gospel for two years. Paul will end his life as an apostle in the same way he had begun it — as a carrier of the Word. His example reminds us of the deep courage that marked the first Apostles. The hostility that surrounded them was from Church and State. Through their efforts the Gospel became deeply lodged in a number of communities. We have kept their memoirs and letters as a reminder forever of that early and fresh faith which spread like wildfire throughout the known world. We too are carriers of that fire.

With this scene of Paul in Rome, Luke has shown how the Gospel moved from Jerusalem to the Eternal City.

Gospel Reading

Peter proceeded to follow the Lord physically, ultimately even unto death. As he moves ahead he notices the Beloved Disciple, whose message is preserved in the Fourth Gospel, following as well. He asks about his fate. The Lord shifts the issue to the importance of Peter's discipleship. These words of Jesus gave birth to a rumor that the Beloved Disciple, last to die, was not to have died until His return. As this Gospel reading ends, we are reminded of the many ways we are called to follow the Lord. We do not know how the Beloved Disciple died. We do not have any witness of his death. We do have the witness of his life. That is enshrined for us in the Fourth Gospel which remains one of the most profound and haunting of the biblical books. There are many ways of serving the Lord both in death and in life. In whatever happens, we are servants of the Lord.

Point

There are many ways of giving witness to the Lord.

OBLIGATORY MEMORIALS

January 2   BASIL THE GREAT AND GREGORY NAZIANZEN

Both of these Doctors of the Church lived around the year 350. Together with Basil's younger brother, Gregory of Nyssa, they comprise the Cappadocian Fathers. Basil was the founder of Eastern monasticism much as Benedict is considered the founder of Western monasticism. Basil tried to restore some measure of harmony among bishops after the acrimonious Arian controversy. The theological importance of the Cappadocians comes from their precision in articulating a theology of the Holy Spirit who, Basil asserted, "with the Father and Son is worshipped and glorified." Basil was the administrator, Gregory the preacher and Gregory of Nyssa the theologian of "three hypostases (persons) in one essence." Their significance lies in the theological location they gave to the Holy Spirit as well as the battles they fought over faith and jurisdiction.

January 4   ELIZABETH ANN SETON

This feast has a unique opening prayer which praises Elizabeth Seton as "wife and mother." She is the only native American saint — born two years before our Declaration of Independence. Baptized an Episcopalian, she was somewhat of a socialite until her husband lost his wealth and later died of tuberculosis. She subsequently converted to Catholicism, started a school in Baltimore and founded the "Sisters of Charity" in Emmitsburg, Maryland. Her children were not great saints by any means and were a cross to her. During her life, she had no visions or mystical transports. She was a caring, sensitive, intelligent, typically American woman. She died of tuberculosis at the age of 46.

January 5   JOHN NEUMANN

John Neumann lived in the mid 1800's and is famous for trying to get prayer and Bible reading out of the public schools. In those days, public schools were, in effect, Protestant schools. Catholic children were punished for not participating in the Protestant services. John Neumann began to build parochial schools. Born in Europe, he was ordained for the diocese of New York State and served as a missionary throughout Western New York. He later joined the Redemptorists and became bishop of Philadelphia which included Delaware, New Jersey and half of Pennsylvania. He started the practice of "Forty Hours" in his diocese, fought lay trusteeism and died of a heart attack at age 49. Typically American in his style of holiness, he had no great ecstasies. He simply cared for people and tried to establish structures to meet human need.

January 17   ANTHONY, ABBOT

Anthony renounced his inheritance to live a solitary life in the desert around the 300's. He returned to the city periodically to fight Arians. His lifestyle of solitary prayer and asceticism provided one of the major influences for the early development of monasticism. Most of what is known about him and the tremendous temptations he resisted in such a solitary life comes to us from a life of Anthony written by Saint Athanasius.

January 21   AGNES

A great deal of legend surrounds this early Roman martyr. She was a beautiful young girl around the year 300 who refused to submit to the desires of Roman libertines and was tortured to death. She represents the vast number of Christians in any age who remain fiercely loyal to their baptismal promises at enormous personal cost. As we sadly learn today, martyrdom is not the prerogative of adults.

This is the day when lambs are blessed by the Pope. Their wool is later used to make the pallia.

January 24 FRANCIS DE SALES

Francis de Sales is a Doctor of the Church. He lived in France in the 1600's. He had been a lawyer and, upon becoming a priest and later bishop, turned to the work of evangelizing the French people whose faith had been eroded by Calvinism. His method was to write and distribute popular religious tracts — an innovative use of what we would call the "media." He is the patron saint of journalists. He is most renowned for his down-to-earth spirituality in the *Introduction to the Devout Life* and the *Treatise on the Love of God.* In these books, he describes the daily life of an average person of any profession who tries to take discipleship seriously. He presented a practical, workable spirituality. His beatification was the very first to take place in Saint Peter's Basilica.

January 25 CONVERSION OF SAINT PAUL

The first reading describes Paul's conversion experience. A "Damascus experience" has become synonymous with sudden change. But it was not a change that sprang from nowhere. Paul had heard Stephen's last words and had contact with the early Christian movement. The seed had been sown. Slowly, the pressure built within him like an internal Mount St. Helens until it finally exploded into his consciousness. His own unrest and the Lord's voice made a perfect fit. We can never tell the effect of the seeds we plant by word and example.

Today's Gospel reading repeats the Lord's mandate to take the Gospel to all creation. This involves much more than revival tents and door to door canvassing. It involves a communication of values. To take the Gospel to all creation is not simply to transmit a book or doctrine. It is to impart a way of life, a Christian awareness of God and a way of viewing human relationships. Our life style is the greatest tool of evangelization — more powerful than a million-watt television station. This is one reason Paul always pointed to his life style as a vivid kind of Gospel lesson.

The conversion of Paul or of any person, is the result of many seeds planted by many people, perhaps unknowingly, by word and example. We can never predict the full effect of the seeds we sow.

January 26   TIMOTHY AND TITUS

Timothy and Titus, addressees of New Testament letters, were Paul's co-workers. They were presbyters or, perhaps, bishops. We do not have a very precise conception of offices in the early Church. In the Gospel reading, Jesus appoints a "further seventy-two." They were not Apostles but evidently were more than ordinary disciples. What is clear to us is that there was a great deal of fluidity in the early Church; they had no difficulty in creating new offices and functions when needed.

There is only one Priest — Jesus Christ. Bishops participate fully in the priestly ministry of Jesus. A portion of that priesthood is communicated to priests and deacons. These three orders together comprise the sacramental expression of the priesthood of Jesus Christ.

In addition, all Christians share in the priesthood of the Lord because we all participate in His great work of reconciliation. Paul had described the many gifts given to the Church: preaching, teaching, administration, service. In the past, all of these gifts were seen to be wrapped into the priesthood whom everyone else assisted. Today, Church law and theology see the priest as an enabler, bringing forth the gifts that are distributed among the people of the parish. Even today, new offices are created to meet new needs. This is one reason for the growth of ministries.

Jesus sent the Eleven and He sent the seventy-two. We are all given our special way of extending Christ to others. Each of us has his or her own role in the work of harvesting.

January 28 THOMAS AQUINAS

Aquinas is known today as the symbol of universally approved orthodoxy. But, three years after his death, he was condemned by the Bishop of Paris in 1277 for "profanity, novelty and materialism." He came from a wealthy family and joined the brand new Dominican order. Until then, roving monks who wandered away from their monasteries were excoriated by Church authorities. Now, Franciscans and Dominicans were established specifically to wander around to meet the needs of a mobile population. Thomas taught at the University of Paris. At this time, people were fascinated by the newly discovered writings of Aristotle. Aquinas sought to link the conclusions of the pagan Aristotle with Christian faith. He was violently opposed by traditionalist Franciscans whose theology was that of Saint Augustine with a heavy overlay of Plato.

Aquinas died at the age of 50. His written legacy is prodigious. His popularity waxed and waned until he was given strong endorsement by Pope Leo XIII, the Code of Canon Law and Vatican II. There are many spiritual descendants of Aquinas who try to do in our day what he attempted to do in the thirteenth century — integrate faith and the modern mind.

Aquinas showed that intelligence is not an intruder into the domain of faith. The same man who wrote the rigorous and subtle theology of the Summa also wrote deeply moving eucharistic hymns such as the *Pange Lingua, Adoro Te, Panis Angelicus* and the old Office of the Feast of Corpus Christi.

January 31   JOHN BOSCO

John Bosco, who died in 1888, is most well-known for his work with youth. He was the "Father Flanagan" of Italy. Rather than simply punish delinquents, he sought to teach them a trade so that they might become productive members of society. He was not an advocate of corporal punishment but sought to appeal to the self-respect that every human being cherishes. He founded a religious congregation under the patronage of Saint Francis de Sales called the Salesians.

February 2   THE PRESENTATION OF THE LORD

Candlemas is a gentle feast of light in the darkness of winter. It reminds us of the Light that has entered the world. In the first reading, the prophet Malachi awaits the coming of the messenger of the Day of the Lord. That messenger may have been an historical personage close to Malachi's time. We know him as John the Baptist. Suddenly, Malachi envisions the coming of the Lord with power and glory to purify and cleanse so that a perfect sacrifice may once again be offered in Jerusalem.

The second reading is the pivot of today's feast. It shows the great high priesthood of Jesus to consist in the linkage between God and humanity as it really is. The Judge awaited by Malachi would view the world through human eyes.

In the Gospel reading, we have old man Simeon, the embodiment of Israel's waiting. He never wavered in his trust in the words of the prophets. Now, before his eyes, the ancient promises come true. He had seen the great Messiah in a thoroughly unexpected way — as a baby. This is how the splendor of God would appear in the darkness — through a gurgling baby. The Messiah would come from and remain with the human family.

The candles we bless at Candlemas are sacramentals. In moments of loneliness, decision, prayer or searching, we might light one of them in our homes to remind us of the abiding presence of the Lord. European custom lit the blessed candle during natural storms. The candle did not make the storm go away but it reminded people that the Lord was with them in the storm. In our personal storms, it is a comforting practice to light the blessed candle to recall that the Light is with us in any darkness.

February 5   AGATHA

Legend surrounds Agatha — another Roman girl martyred for preserving her physical and spiritual integrity. She is mentioned in the Roman Canon and had a great devotional following in the early Church. Many saints gave their lives for the Lord in that early era. Many had local remembrances among a few friends or perhaps a heroic holiness known only within their families. Their real virtue is secure with the Lord. It will not be lost.

February 6   PAUL MIKI AND HIS COMPANIONS

Twenty-six Jesuit and Franciscan priests, brothers and Christian laymen were among these first martyrs in Nagasaki. The shoguns blew hot and cold about Christianity. These men were caught in the crossfire of the high politics that dominated European relations with Japan in the 1500's. They were crucified in an especially brutal way. The Gospel and its martyrs had found a way into Japan.

February 10   SCHOLASTICA

Scholastica, who lived about 540, was the sister of Saint
Benedict and the first Benedictine nun. All we know of her is a
story of Benedict's annual visit with her. As he was ready to
depart, she prayed that a storm would force him to remain
longer. After the storm subsided, he returned to the monastery.
Three days later, he realized that she had died when he saw a
dove fly to heaven. This tiny story reminds us of the precious
gift which the presence of other people is to us. Many people
are like landmarks in our lives. We take them for granted and
when they are gone, we are somewhat left off-balance. The
story of Scholastica teaches the lesson of appreciation of the
many gifts we have received from God in the person of other
human beings.

February 14   CYRIL AND METHODIUS

These brothers from the 800's are called the Apostles to
the Slavic peoples. It was a time of East-West tension between
Pope and Patriarch. Cyril and Methodius preached and imple-
mented an Eastern style liturgy while encouraging the people to
remain faithful to Rome. The Russian Cyrillic alphabet is based
on an alphabet devised by Cyril.

They come to our day representing the importance of a
liturgy that speaks intelligibly to people, ecumenism among
various traditions within the Church and a fidelity to the Holy
Father that does not negate indigenous national pride and
traditions.

February 22   CHAIR OF PETER

This feast celebrates apostolic authority which is deriva-
tive from apostolic witness. What the Apostles saw and handed

on has become the core of what we call our apostolic tradition. Very often, the "apostolic tradition" is shrunken into an emphasis on doctrine alone. It is a great deal more than that. The Apostles handed on a power and a way of life.

In the first reading, Peter reminds the elders to be examples to their flock. The successors to the Apostles are to show the way of Christian resolution of conflict, forgiveness and concern for the marginal people. It is very easy to delimit the apostolic witness to doctrine which can be encapsulated in a catechism. We transmit a great deal more by what we are than by what we say. What a priest does when he leaves the pulpit is as telling as the words he has spoken. Our message to the world is shown by how we deal with each other and with the problems of life. Our life, in fact, shows what we really believe. We preach what we practice.

The "keys of the kingdom" given to Peter can lock people out but can also be used to let people into the experience of the Lord's reign. Our greatest attraction to the world lies not in our theory but in our existence as a community. We can be one place where the law of the jungle does not dominate, where people can come to see how those who believe Jesus to be the Messiah live and deal with each other.

February 23 POLYCARP

Polycarp, a disciple of John, was a martyr in the year 150. He was about 85 years old when he became a victim of mob rule and went to his death with great dignity and heroism. The account of his martyrdom is among the earliest "lives of the saints."

March 7 PERPETUA AND FELICITY

A diary kept by the noblewoman Perpetua recorded the

events of their martyrdom around the year 200. Perpetua was a new mother and Felicity, her slave, was with child. They died heroically. Despite their different income brackets, social levels and races, they were bonded in their love of and witness to the Lord Jesus. Their faith united them in life and in death.

March 19   JOSEPH

The word "faith" can mean various things. It can mean the content of belief but also has the more fundamental meaning of "trust" as when a person has faith in another individual or in God.

Today's readings give two examples of faith as trust in God. The first is the example of the old man Abraham. He was well on in years when he was called to leave his homeland, to be the father of a child of great promise and to be tested on Mount Moriah. He is called our "father in faith." He is the father of all who trust in God.

Our second example is that of a young man in his twenties — Joseph. He cared for Mary and Jesus, supported and protected them. He was also a man of faith.

Great demands were made on Abraham and Joseph. They trusted in God and great things were done through their faith. The dynasty God promised to David came true under the watchful, loving eye of Joseph in his deep love for Mary.

Our lives take strange and bizarre turns. It takes great faith to realize that God is working out His purpose through us. Salvation history continues even as we speak. Each of us is an unfinished chapter in that story. Each of us, as did Abraham and Joseph, sets into motion a string of causes and effects on other people. Some part of the world is actually different because we are here. The end result is hidden from us. For now, like Abraham and Joseph, we can only trust God that everything is unfolding as it should.

March 25   ANNUNCIATION

There are two major cycles in the liturgical year. The first and oldest is Easter which includes Lent and the weeks of the Easter season. The other cycle is Christmas which includes Advent and the weeks of the Christmas season. Today's celebration of the Announcement of Christ, when Jesus was conceived, is exactly nine months before Christmas Day. It takes place in Lent — an unusual intersection of the two great cycles.

It reminds us that we have come a long way from Bethlehem. Then, we had angels, shepherds, wise men — all talking of the future and the great destiny of this baby. Now, in Lent, the baby has become a man. The Gospel readings become ominous. The tension is acute. At the Annunciation, Mary was perhaps nineteen. On Good Friday, she is past fifty. We are approaching the day for which the baby was born. The celebration of Christmas only makes sense in the light of Easter.

Today's feast reminds us that the great events of the Triduum can be traced to a very simple beginning. A young girl said "Yes" to the Lord.

The same is true of our achievements in the spiritual life. The great experiences of God's presence, purpose and call can be traced to very simple beginnings: a moment of prayer, simple words of promise between two people at an altar — and from these simple moments come a life of faithfulness to God, a lifelong marriage and a Christian family.

During this time of Lent, we might keep in mind that although heroic deeds make the books and the lives of the saints, those great accomplishments are made possible by the simple but fundamental events of prayer, Mass and Eucharist. Lent is a time to examine not necessarily how heroic we might become but how faithful we are in simple things. Like prayer, promises and concern for others, these simple things are full of redemption and saving power.

April 7   JOHN BAPTIST DE LA SALLE

John de la Salle lived in France in the late 1600's. He became interested in the education of the poor and gradually founded the Christian Brothers. He was innovative in his development of teaching techniques. A great many controversies and lawsuits plagued his life as a priest. To avoid a caste system in the congregation he founded, he ruled that no brother should ever become a priest and that no priest ever be allowed to join the congregation. Today, the Christian Brothers are among the largest teaching orders in the Church.

April 11   STANISLAUS OF CRACOW

Pope John Paul II made this feast an obligatory memorial for the universal Church. Stanislaus was bishop of Cracow in Poland about the year 1000. He opposed the political and sexual excesses of the king, Boleslaus. While other bishops were afraid to take an anti-government position, Stanislaus was forthright. He excommunicated the king. In return, the king had him killed. Stanislaus is patron of Poland.

April 25   MARK

There is not much that we know about Mark, the patron saint of Venice. His Gospel is the shortest, oldest and bluntest of the Gospels. He had been an aide to Peter and a friend of Paul. He wrote his Gospel for Christians who were disappointed at the delay of the Second Coming and fearful of the virulent persecution waged against them. The center of Mark's Gospel is, appropriately, the words of the Lord: "If a man wishes to come after me, he must deny his very self, take up his cross and follow."

Discipleship and the cross form the twin themes of Mark's

Gospel. Today's first reading shows him to be a companion of the Apostles. He had had a falling-out and then a reconciliation with Paul. Some say he founded a church and died for the faith. There is little else we know about him. What we do know is that he did not spend his entire life writing the Gospel. There is a great deal we do not know about most people. There are only snapshots that we see. The rest is invisible to us but completely visible to God.

What we offer to God is not a deathbed prayer but a lifetime. The Lord looks at our life to see how well we have followed His command to preach to the ends of the earth and to root the message into our hearts.

April 29 CATHERINE OF SIENA

Catherine of Siena was an unusually vivid personality from the 1300's. The fourteenth century was a brutal time. Wars were fought all over; the plague had decimated a third of Europe; the Pope was at Avignon. She was the last of 23 children. She had asked her father for her own room and got it. She was a young girl of strong visions. She had once imagined herself to be a bride of Christ at a wedding attended by Mary, John, Paul, and Dominic with music supplied by David. (We can see why she got her own room.) She was a woman of spiritual common sense and attracted a discussion group that came to her home for spiritual conversation. The neighbors were not patient with such novelty as young men were coming in and out at all hours.

Her advice was later sought by people in high places. She was used as an intermediary by kings and generals and managed to persuade the Pope to return to Rome. Six volumes of her correspondence remain.

She died at the age of 33. She is co-patron of Italy. Her life shows us that criticism of the Church is not identical with disloyalty. Furthermore, her eccentricities give proof to the Lord's words that "in My Father's house, there are many mansions." She was an unusual personality, assertive and bright — those very attributes enabled her to stand out and influence the politics of her time. Holiness and loyalty to the Church can take many forms.

May 2   ATHANASIUS

Arianism thrived in the 300's. It was a complicated movement that implicated politics, personalities and a little bit of theology. In Egypt, a priest named Arius taught that Jesus was not completely identical with God. That tore the Church apart. The emperor convened the Council of Nicaea which began the process of hammering out a creed. The doctrinal resolution of the Council settled little practically. Arians and Anti-Arians continued to battle. Athanasius was at the heart of the controversy. Six times he was sent into exile. In fact, he spent half of his episcopal career in exile. After he died, the Council of Constantinople finalized what we call the Nicene Creed.

Athanasius seems somewhat fanatical in our time when we are used to composing differences. This issue was so central for him that he would allow no compromise. The nature of Jesus was absolutely crucial to what salvation was all about. Either God was in Jesus from the very start, or not. If not, God remains detached from the human scene. If God was in Jesus, the distance is bridged.

May 3   PHILIP AND JAMES

This is James "the less" or "the younger." Philip is a Greek name. James was head of the Jerusalem Church and was martyred in the year 62. He had sought an accommodation between the conservative Jewish Christians and the Gentile

Christians. The crafting of the decree of the Jerusalem Church was largely due to him. We know Philip from John's Gospel.

We celebrate the Apostles because they are our link to history. They remind us that the events we bring to life in our liturgy are not mythological. As the first reading reports, Jesus walked the earth and was seen after His Resurrection by the Eleven. They saw His gestures and heard His words.

The second reason why the Apostles are important is that they were the very first to interpret the meaning of the events of Good Friday and Easter Sunday. It was "for our sins." The life of Jesus was a great deal more than an ordinary human life. Over the centuries, all kinds of interpretations of the significance of Jesus would be developed. The apostolic witness as articulated in the New Testament remains normative for all Christians.

Finally, by preaching and teaching, they enabled others who did not see the gestures and hear the words to experience the Risen Lord in Word and Sacrament. They created the liturgical experience of Christ and were the first to celebrate in memory of Him.

But the Apostles were very human. In today's Gospel reading, as the Lord declares Himself to be the Way, Philip still asks to see the Father. He wanted to witness the glory and majesty descend from heaven. Jesus answers that whoever has seen and experienced Him has seen and experienced the Father. The Apostles are a comforting reminder to us that holiness is humanly possible. In our mistakes and failures, the humanity of the Church is live testimony to the fact that the Lord loves us and not some ideal. He died for us, just as we are.

May 14   MATTHIAS

All we know of Matthias is found in today's first reading. In fact, with the exceptions of Peter and Paul, we know very little about most of the Twelve.

In this first reading, Peter speaks of the design of God that was operative in the events they had witnessed. Judas must be replaced because there must be Twelve in time for Pentecost. The requirements for Judas' successor were not only that he have been a witness of the Risen Christ but also of the Lord's public ministry from the baptism of John. The life and Resurrection of Jesus are inseparable. They are mutually interpretative. Matthias was chosen by lottery.

As the Apostles died after Pentecost, they were not replaced. It was impossible to replace eyewitnesses. After their death, the link to them became important. As variant doctrines arose from many quarters, the acid test of the authentic way of Jesus became apostolic doctrine, apostolic faith, apostolic creed and apostolic succession.

The Gospel reading reminds us that there is more to being apostolic than an apostolic connection. That our historical genealogy can be traced to apostolic times shows historical legitimacy but we cannot rest on our apostolic link alone. The Lord speaks to the entire Church in saying, "Love one another. . ." If we go to a physician to be healed, the degrees on his office wall are an important qualification. The more important requirement we have is that he be able to do some healing. This is the other side of apostolicity. We must show that we continue the work of Jesus' healing and loving. The great draw of the Church is less its antiquity than its continuation of the ministry of Jesus. Jesus lives and heals through us.

May 26   PHILIP NERI

Philip Neri lived about 400 years ago in the late 1500's. Tired of the commercialism and lack of Christian principle he saw in his uncle's business, he fled to Rome. In those days, that was similar to a person who hates crowds fleeing to Manhattan. After seventeen years as a layman, he was ordained a priest and established small prayer and study groups called oratories where religious services and discussions were held. Music written for these groups were called "oratorios." He established a congregation of diocesan priests called Oratorians. They take no vows but live a common life. He converted many people who were influential in Church government. Hence, his title of Apostle of Rome.

May 31 VISITATION

The visitation scene carried a great deal more theological power for the early Christians than it does for us. It does carry an important and timeless message. The sequence of events is important. After the Annunciation, Mary visits Elizabeth and only afterwards does she sing the Magnificat, the song of gratitude and joy.

There is a special sense of intense praise a person feels after the joy of faith has been shared with another. We need such sharing. Whether we share a joke, a complaint or the details of our pain, basic human emotions need to be communicated. This is especially true in our spiritual lives.

The second reason to share is validation. We need another person to say of our achievement or gift, "Yes, it is real." Paul reminds us to rejoice with the happy and weep with the sorrowing. People need to be told they are doing well and that what they are doing is important and valuable. The Pope needs it; bishops need it; everyone needs it. After Mary realizes that she is to give birth to the Holy One, she goes *immediately* to Elizabeth. To assist the older woman? To share the news? Only afterwards does she sing her song of joy.

It is painful to live with an unshared vision, an unacknowledged achievement, a misunderstood gift. The pain of loneliness lies not in physical isolation but in the assumption that nobody cares. Growth in faith is a road that each of us has to walk on his or her own. No one can do the walking for us. But we do not have to walk alone. We should encourage each other along the way.

June   SACRED HEART

The feast of the Sacred Heart was once a major feast. It was a double of the second class with its own octave. The devotion was widespread: leagues of the Sacred Heart, First Friday devotions, Consecration and Enthronement of the Sacred Heart, the Sacred Heart program and magazine, the Apostleship of Prayer and a great deal more. So much of this devotion is gone but what it sought to instill in us remains. In a way, it is a victim of its own success.

The devotion grew enormously popular during the reign of Louis XIV. It was a reaction against a Jansenism which taught that grace was given to few; we were all corrupt and unworthy of a God too holy for us. Communion became infrequent. The Jesuits responded to this by encouraging the Sacred Heart devotion to show that Jesus loves every one of us. The emphasis was on the heart — an ancient symbol of the innermost reality of a person. "To Jesus Heart all burning with fervent love for men (and women)." The reception of communion was emphasized at least on the First Friday of each month.

Today's first reading from the severe Book of Deuteronomy emphasizes God's abiding love. The second reading from John speaks of the Lord's love for us. The Gospel reading from Matthew recalls the words of the Lord to the weary that they come to Him.

The Sacred Heart devotion tells us today that Jesus has real love for us. That means He can be hurt by our rejection. Karl Rahner, a Jesuit theologian, once remarked that if we have loved someone indifferent to us, we have the grace of devotion to the Sacred Heart. We can then understand the heart of Christ.

The Sacred Heart means that Jesus has a love that reaches out to everyone. It means that He has a real love that can change us. Just as our realization that we are loved by another can transform our perception of the world, so an appreciation of the Lord's love for us can enable us to feel the horror of sin as well as the value the Lord places on us. His is a love that heals, forgives, makes whole and never dies.

June 1   JUSTIN MARTYR

Justin was a martyr in more ways than one. He lived around 150. He was a professional philosopher who glided from school to school. Finally, he recounts a moving story of his conversion to the Christian faith through an old man who told him about Jesus and the Old Testament prophets.

Justin was the first major intellectual defender of the faith. He presented a justification for Christian belief to show it to be reasonable and not irrational. In his day, it was an effort to show the compatibility between the philosophy of Plato and revelation. His effort was as shocking to some people as would be the attempt today to show the compatibility between the Gospel and Freud or Marx.

Justin's second claim to fame is an early description of the Roman liturgy which he provides in one of his defenses of Christianity. It is the earliest description we have.

Today's first reading highlights faith as the floor on which theology is built and not vice versa. At the cross, we are all equal. All of us take our own experience of Christ and the cross and express and apply it as best we can. Intellectuals such as Justin do it in their own way. Missionaries like Paul do so in their way. Each of us applies the mystery of the cross in his or her own way.

June 3   CHARLES LWANGA AND COMPANIONS

They are called proto-martyrs. They are the first canonized martyrs of sub-Saharan Africa. They refused the homosexual advances of the Ugandan king and were martyred about a century ago.

June 5   BONIFACE

Called the Apostle of Germany, Boniface was a powerful teacher, preacher and missionary statesman who single-handedly established the administrative structure of the Church in Germany. The most famous incident of his early missionary work was his chopping down a tree sacred to a pagan god. He went from being an active missionary to being an administrator and back to being a missionary in his old age when he was martyred about 750.

June 11   BARNABAS

Barnabas was Paul's companion. He sold his farm and gave the proceeds to the Apostles as he entered the young Christian community. He was so intimately involved with Paul's work that he is called an "Apostle." His home base, as seen in today's first reading, was in Antioch where he was part of the great outreach to the Gentiles.

June 13   ANTHONY OF PADUA

Anthony has become so popular and effective as a finder of lost articles that we forget the details of his life. He joined the Franciscan order during the life of Saint Francis around 1220. He taught theology, was a great preacher and is a Doctor of the Church (his statues show him holding a book). His preaching was said to work physical as well as moral miracles. He returned to Padua where he died at the age of 36 and was canonized a year later. His love for the poor is captured in the custom of the distribution of Saint Anthony's Bread.

June 21   ALOYSIUS GONZAGA

Aloysius is an unusual saint who came from a family of villains. Perhaps his intense sanctity was in reaction to the treachery he saw around him. Some of his devotional exercises were extreme but that is a function of his young age. Many young people find a point of unity in their life and become extreme in expressing their dedication to it. He became a Jesuit novice and died while tending the sick during a plague in 1591. He is a patron of Catholic youth.

June 24   BIRTH OF JOHN THE BAPTIST

John the Baptist was a revered figure in the early Church. In the Middle Ages, hundreds of religious groups and churches were placed under his patronage. Many followers of the Lord had originally been disciples of the Baptist. Many remained followers of the Baptist even after his death.

John represents the continual need we have for repentance to prepare for the irruption of God's presence into our lives. Secondly, John's whole mission in life was to point the way to Christ. That is very much the heart of the Christian vocation. Paul tells us that John set the stage. Isaiah speaks about a mysterious suffering servant which the Church has always identified as Christ but which we take here as referring to John as well. "I called you . . . though you thought it was all in vain . . . now you will have glory through me."

Each of us is created for a purpose. Our genes come from our parents. Our unique identity comes from God. We can never list all the events we set in motion. Like John, we bring people to the light in ways we cannot anticipate. If we carry a burden, experience a tragedy or have seen the seamy side of life — these can be ways that we are able to connect with others. We all have the power to enlarge the lives of others, heal their wounds and assist them through complex problems.

June 28   IRENAEUS

Irenaeus lived around the year 200. He was a saint and a martyr. He is unusually important because with him we see Catholicism emerge in a form we can recognize. To this point, the Christian movement is in a somewhat fluid state. Each area seemed to have its own theology. All kinds of "sacred books" were in use. There were many wandering preachers. Irenaeus places emphasis upon apostolic authority — historical connectedness with the Apostles; a creed — a set of core beliefs; and a rudimentary canon of Scripture — certain recognized books — as guarantees of an authentic Christian way. These emerge as the defining characteristics of early Catholicism.

Theologically, he opposed the sharp dualism of the Gnostics through the arresting notion of *anakephaliosis* — everything, matter and spirit, is summed up (recapitulated) in Christ.

June 29   PETER AND PAUL

Each has his own basilica in Rome. This is an old feast because it commemorates the death of neither Peter nor Paul. It comes from the 300's to recall a day when a joint feast was established.

Peter and Paul represent two complementary dimensions of the Church. Peter maintains the traditions; Paul represents the drive to adapt, expand and amplify the Gospel. Peter is the centripetal force that seeks the center; Paul is the centrifugal force that reaches to embrace different cultures and perhaps, one day, different planets.

The Church needs both. Without the centering of Peter, the Church would have been a loose collection of fragmented sects. Without the expansive force of Paul, the Church would have stayed a Jewish group in Jerusalem.

The same is true of our spiritual lives. Peter holds us to our center — the core of our faith which is our relationship with Christ. Our baptismal link with the Lord is the rock that anchors all the changes of our life. With Paul, we gather new insights and new understandings of discipleship and of our Lord. Sometimes, we develop new spiritual practices as the seasons of our life change.

What is true of the Church is true of our individual selves: we have to change to keep our ancient faith a living thing.

July 3   THOMAS THE APOSTLE

Many legends surround the later life of "doubting Thomas" that have been kept for us in the apocryphal "Acts of Thomas." Still, there is a group of Christians (the Malabar rite) that traces itself back to Thomas.

The famous scene in today's Gospel reading sums up John's Gospel. Thomas sees the Risen Lord and affirms, "My Lord and my God" — the words of an ancient creed. The Lord then says to him and to all Christians that those who have not seen the Risen Lord but have believed in the sacramental presence of Christ are blessed.

This incident of the doubts of Thomas carries two messages for us. First, his doubts were intensified by his isolation from the community. When he returned to the apostolic community he again found his faith. Often, when we have doubts about our faith, we tend to isolate ourselves instead of seeking to share them with another to resolve them. The second point is

that seeing is not identical with faith. Many people saw Jesus
during His life but did not believe. Many saw miracles, such as
that of the loaves, and failed to understand them. Faith is the
judgment and assurance that the Risen Lord is with us in
different forms — through sign, gesture, word and Spirit.

Doubt can lead to deeper faith and through that faith to
contact with the Risen Lord.

July 11   BENEDICT

The early Christians, supported by their strong belief in an
imminent end of the world, followed a strict and rigorous life
style. When the end failed to come, the Church became part of
the establishment. As a result, many Christians began to search
for a simpler life style and fled the city to the desert. These were
the "desert fathers," some of whom were prone to ascetic
excesses. Other Christians lived in communities under a rule of
obedience and the general supervisory authority of the local
bishop. Unfortunately, some local bishops used these local
monks as the equivalent of what we would call "goon squads"
to punish heretics.

Benedict was convinced that there must be a middle
ground in the monastic life between excessive individual aus-
terity and membership in goon squads. In the mid-500's, he
eventually founded a monastery at Monte Cassino known for
its moderation. Benedict was a practical man. He was neither
excessively speculative nor ascetic. Moderation and balance
remain hallmarks of Benedictine spirituality.

Pope Gregory the Great helped the Benedictine order to
spread and multiply.

July 15   BONAVENTURE

Bonaventure is a Doctor of the Church. He was minister

general of the Franciscan Order and later was made a cardinal. He lived around 1250. He is sometimes called the "second founder of the Franciscan Order." The thirteenth century, called the "best" of centuries by some, was a turbulent time. Dozens of theological systems abounded. Among them was the Franciscan school which was made up of a strange collection of people. Its left wing included the great scholar Roger Bacon, whom some ignorantly accused of black magic. Bonaventure represented the conservative wing of the Franciscan school. If Aquinas plots the way of the intellect to God, Bonaventure speaks of the heart and love as avenues to the Lord. He saw the world as filled with traces (vestigia) of God. It is God who enables us to even think about Him. In his famous *Journey of the Mind to God,* Bonaventure writes, "If you ask how mystical experience is possible, look to the grace of God and not to doctrine, to the thrust of the heart and not the intellect, to prayer and not to research, seek the Lover and not the Teacher . . . look not to the light of the intellect but to the burning fire that carries the soul to God."

July 22   MARY MAGDALENE

Mary Magdalene has become known as the paradigmatic sinner of the New Testament. Seven devils were cast from her. She is a case study in conversion.

Contrition is sorrow for sin. We deviate from the way we should be living although the general direction of our life is on the right track. Conversion is much more profound and drastic. It involves a complete shift in orientation, a 180 degree change, and a change from the inside out.

In today's first reading, Paul speaks about a new creation. This is the transforming experience of God that reshapes a person's center. That re-creation affects the rest of our life. This is what Mary Magdalene has come to represent: an experience of God so profound that it is like being born all over again. It is not cosmetic change.

In today's Gospel reading, the Magdalene is the first person to see the Lord after His Resurrection. A convert was the first witness to the Risen Lord. Jesus' instruction that she stop clinging to Him reminds us that our new ties with the Risen Lord are deep and remain with us wherever we go. It also reminds us to share our experience with others.

July 25   JAMES

This is James "the Greater" — the older. Legend has him travelling to Spain. The shrine of Saint James at Compostella was one of the three great places of pilgrimage in the Middle Ages.

The Apostles have a special place in the Church as privileged witnesses of the Lord. We have given them a superhuman status akin to the Founding Fathers of the United States. Yet, the Gospels are almost brutal in their characterization of the Apostles as slow in getting the point. They are often no different than the uncomprehending crowds. Two incidents involve James the Greater. He is called a Son of Thunder by the Lord because he wanted to rain fire and brimstone on Samaritan towns that refused to greet Jesus. The second incident is found in today's Gospel reading where his mother seeks a personal distinction for her sons. The Lord's response to her is direct. They shall drink of the same cup of death as He.

Martyrdom comes in many forms. One kind of pain is a realization that we who are commissioned by the Lord carry a treasure, as Paul reminds us, in earthen vessels. Our personality can turn people away from the Gospel and the Church. On the other hand, our ordinary human experiences can become vehicles for God's grace and power as well. We all carry a treasure in earthen vessels.

We are frequently praised in the Church as being "the people of God." Yet, we know our shortcomings and frailties very well. This does not mean that we lack the Holy Spirit. We can apply Paul's message to ourselves and to the weaknesses of the Apostles. We carry this treasure in earthen vessels to make clear that its power comes from God. The Holy Spirit is not carried about in golden monstrances but in tupperware.

July 26   JOACHIM AND ANNE

Most of what we know about the parents of Mary comes from the *Protoevangelium of James,* a devotional tract revered in the early Church which never was made part of Scripture. It describes the Conception, Birth and Presentation of Mary.

Today's first reading applies the words of Sirach to Joachim and Anne. After describing the glory of God seen in nature, Sirach describes the glory of God found in people. These were the people faithful to the Old Testament promises. They were the remnant threaded through history who were the connecting link between the faith of Abraham and the birth of Jesus Christ. Joachim and Anne were part of that remnant.

The Gospel reading reminds us that these Old Testament figures remained faithful while all they had were promises. We read the same Old Testament promises but see them fulfilled in Jesus. We now have the Holy Spirit and the Body and Blood of the Lord as permanent gifts. The immortality of which Sirach wrote was the immortality of family and reputation. This is one reason why childlessness and an early death were Old Testament disasters. Jesus enabled us to look past death toward an eternal personal existence. What the Old Testament saw in shadow we can see clearly.

Just as the faith of Joachim and Anne lived on in Mary and, in that way, their faith actually helped to bring about the fulfillment of the very promises in which they trusted, so our faith lives on in people we know well and helps to bring about the public reign of Christ for which we pray.

July 29   MARTHA

Martha did all the work. Instinctively, most of us side with her. She represents all those people in any parish who keep things going, oil the wheels, do the mimeographing, keep lists, empty ashtrays, fix cracks in the plaster and fold chairs after an event. Martha reminds us that all of those very practical tasks are also ways of showing and sharing love. Martha and Mary really represent two dimensions of every personality. Martha represents all those things that go into the business of living. Mary focuses for us the times of prayer and quiet when we can pull it all together in the Lord. Both are necessary. Without Martha, Mary would starve to death. Without Mary, Martha would forget the point of it all. Martha and Mary: work and prayer. They are two dimensions of every personality, each showing love in its own way.

July 31   IGNATIUS OF LOYOLA

Today's first reading is the source of the Jesuit motto: Ad Majorem Dei Gloriam (AMDG), All for the greater glory of God.

We all know the story of Ignatius. He came from a wealthy Spanish family. He was an educated man and a lukewarm Catholic. His recuperation from a battle wound triggered a conversion experience. He was "born again." He then organized a society of priests modeled on the military. Thus was the "Company of Jesus" born. They have had a turbulent history. They were suppressed by a Pope and threatened by a few more. Despite all of these close calls, the Jesuits are survivors. Many unique features are represented by the Jesuit order.

One of them which we might consider is the approach to God through the intellect and the professions. By their preaching and lives, Jesuits show that no human endeavor or line of work is alien to Christ. There are Jesuit biologists, physicians, lawyers, scientists, economists, philosophers, linguists and theologians. There is no human activity in which the Lord cannot be found or to which He cannot be brought. It is no surprise that many of the great universities of the world have been founded by Jesuits.

One feature of Jesuit spirituality is the thirty-day retreat. It was Ignatius' way of institutionalizing the conversion experience. One does not emerge from it the same way one went in. It is a rigorous time of spiritual basic training. The genius of the Jesuit order is that everything human is seen to be capable of being an extension of Christ's redemptive work.

August 1   ALPHONSUS LIGUORI

Alphonsus lived in the 1700's. He was a lawyer who became a priest. He was an exceptional home missionary whose specialty became moral theology. He worked out a system called Moderate Probabilism which was the most workable of a number of systems used in those days to compute solutions to moral problems. He wrote a Way of the Cross which is still used in some parishes. The Redemptorist order which he founded had a turbulent early history. There were problems with their title to property and authority structure, and they were even accused of being covert Jesuits! The great significance of Alphonsus lies in his effort to make Christian living a practical and realistic way of life.

August 4   JOHN VIANNEY

He is the patron saint of parish priests. Parish priests receive a bad reputation from the media. They are thought to be the "general practitioners" of the Church with none of the flair or expertise of the specialists.

The parish ministry requires a great deal of skill and an application of practical intelligence. To preach a homily each week to a congregation of various ages, problems, marital situations, nationalities and income levels is a great challenge. It is much easier to preach to a homogeneous and select group.

Further, the parish priest is the "point man" where all the programs developed in diocesan offices come home to rest. The programs of the Right to Life group, Youth ministry, Charismatic Prayer Group, Catholics United for the Faith, Liturgy Committee, Holy Name, Vincent de Paul Society, Religious Education, Continuing Adult Education, Altar Society, Choir, Catholic Charities, Scouting, Catholics Against Nuclear War, Sodality, Bingo, Pre-Cana, Marriage Encounter and the Parish Council all come to the desk of the parish priest. He is the one who must coordinate the interests of all these groups with limited parish resources while helping to make their programs operational.

The parish priest is the instrument through which the teaching of the Church and the programs of a bishop come face to face with people. He is the instrument of ultimate persuasion. If the parish priest fails or succeeds, the bishop fails or succeeds. The parish priest is the point of interface between the Church and the world. He is where the healing ministry described in today's Gospel reading continues. The parish priest is the real specialist.

August 6 TRANSFIGURATION

Let us talk about the experience of God.

The Apostles had a powerful experience on that mountain in today's Gospel reading. Up to this point, they have seen the miracles, heard the teaching and seen the gestures. Here, for the very first time, they saw the glory of Christ. It was a moment when the realization that Jesus was Lord burst inside their brain. It hit home. It all clicked. This was a holy event. Their experience of Jesus as Lord was through Jewish eyes, with Moses and Elijah. The Lord had spoken of a suffering Messiah and now they realized that this was the ancient plan of God.

Many of us have had our own experience of Christ. It was probably not as high-pressured as that of the Apostles but we have had our own burning bush. It may have happened long ago, or recently, as we were saying the Rosary, attending a novena, reading the Bible, hearing a homily, jogging. It comes in all kinds of ways. It was a time when we experienced a closeness to the Lord.

If you have not yet had such an experience, there is no gimmick or technique to produce it. It is a gift. But, if you are looking for the Lord, you will find Him. In today's second reading, Peter says, "We were there. If you keep your attention focused on the message then the morning star (Christ) will rise in your heart."

Such moments are extraordinary and do not come often. Times of really deep communion with God or with other people are rare. It is because such moments are extraordinary that we Catholics experience the Lord in a more usual way in the liturgy. The apostolic experience of the Lord was translated into Word and Sacrament. It is here, in this way, that the Lord promised He would always be present. The liturgy is less dramatic than the Transfiguration event but just as real. This too is a holy event.

August 8   DOMINIC

Dominic lived around 1200. The Dominicans and Franciscans were established because of the changing character of the times. Until now, monks were rooted in the soil. They stayed, or were supposed to stay, in a monastery. But the middle class was on the move into towns with the rise of commerce. Dominic established an order for this middle class. These friars did not withdraw from the city but penetrated it as itinerant preachers. Dominic's order was a theological rapid deployment force that opposed various underground types of religiosity. Their keynote is simplicity and learning. They are much more prominent in Europe than they are in the United States. In America they have established Providence College. They are a remarkably democratic order.

August 10   LAWRENCE

The feast of the early Church deacon, Lawrence, is an occasion to consider a quiet revolution that has been taking place in the Church. This is the surge in the number of married deacons in the Church. Their number is rapidly expanding. These men are ordained to the ministry, assigned by the bishop and are engaged in all kinds of apostolates. They are all ages and all professions. They are able to baptize, preach, witness marriages, bury the dead and minister to the sick. The decline in the number of priests, largely due to the decline in the size of the pool of young people from which vocations normally come, has been matched by the rise in the number of permanent deacons. Perhaps they signal the recession of a highly clericalized Church and the beginning of a new and innovative harvest.

The same is true of our own lives. We have our own deaths and resurrections. The Holy Spirit enables us to take moments that look like an end and make these "deaths" the starting point of a new life for us. Something must always die for new life to begin.

The rhythm of the spiritual life is one of death and resurrection — both, not just one or the other.

August 11 CLARE

She was a beautiful Italian girl who lived around 1200 and wished to follow Francis. It was spiritual love at first sight. She took the Franciscan vows and founded the Poor Clares. Francis' own friars were the first order; the Poor Clares were the second order; others who wished to follow the spirit and rule of Francis were called the third order.

August 14 MAXIMILIAN KOLBE

Maximilian Kolbe reminds us that martyrdom is not limited to Roman times. He was a Conventual Franciscan who was light years ahead of anybody else in the use of the media to promote the Christian faith, especially devotion to the Mother of Jesus. He established a city-like structure of friars to publish papers and magazines. His city of the Immaculate was the largest aggregation of Franciscans anywhere on the face of the earth. With the Nazi occupation of Poland, he was taken to Auschwitz where he gave his life in place of another prisoner. In that act, his faith bore its final and greatest fruit. That single act gave greater glory to the power of his faith than all the printing presses in the world.

August 20 BERNARD

Saint Bernard lived around 1100. He became a monk and established the monastery at Clairvaux to return to the original

Benedictine rule. From that monastery came several others. He was a controversialist, poet, theologian, debater, preacher of crusades and a mystic. He was deeply involved in the political and ecclesiastical conflicts of his time. His devotion to the Mother of Jesus is classic.

August 21   PIUS X

Pius X is well known in recent Church history for his rigorous defense of the Catholic faith. In a time when a confusing flood of intellectual currents was sweeping throughout the Western world, Pius realized that critical assimilation of them was impossible. The only summary way of dealing with such a major intellectual crisis was to pull the wagons around. The time for assimilation might come decades later. More important for him was the securing of a sound and clearly defined Catholic identity. To that end, he reformed canon law, the liturgy and the Roman curia.

The achievement for which he is most famous is the encouragement of children to receive communion frequently. Until his time, first communion was popularly received in a person's teen-aged years. Pius allowed younger children after the age of seven to have the opportunity to share in the eucharistic celebration in the fullest possible way. This was a remarkably bold sacramental judgment.

August 22   QUEENSHIP OF MARY

This feast is only about thirty years old. It was established in 1954 to give glory to Mary, the Mother of Jesus. It is an occasion to recall the place of motherhood in the transmission of faith. A great deal of Mary poured into Jesus. This is a feast to recall her faith. Mary's trust in God and her love of Jesus were more significant redemptively than her genetic connection to

Jesus. Her place in heaven which we celebrate today is the triumph of womanhood, faith and simplicity.

August 24 BARTHOLOMEW

We do not know much about Bartholomew (or Nathanael as, inexplicably, he is called in John's Gospel). That fact is significant. It provides an opportunity to consider the role of the Twelve in the early Church. The Twelve did not function precisely as our bishops do today. The fit is not exact. Bishops today have a geographical jurisdiction. The Twelve did not seem to have local geographic dioceses but a general supervisory position of great honor. Much as the immediate associates of Martin Luther King, or our own Founding Fathers were given great deference and honor, the Twelve functioned as guarantors of the tradition handed down about Jesus. They functioned collegially at major moments in the life of the early Church such as the Hellenist crisis of the unattended Greek widows and the later circumcision debate.

We do not know much about them individually except for Peter. As a group, they were the foundation of the renewed Israel (the point of today's first reading). They were the line of continuity between God's people in the Old Testament into the New. Further, they saw with their eyes what the rest of us can experience sacramentally.

There are points of similarity between ourselves and the Twelve. Even though our cultures, languages and vocabularies differ, we continue in the same discipleship, faith and service of the same Risen Lord.

August 27 MONICA

She lived around 350 and is most famous for the tears she shed and the prayers she said for her wayward son Augustine.

Those prayers were answered. She represents the trials of any parent who sees a child traveling down a destructive road. Parents can guide and supervise their children up to a point. There comes a moment when responsibility for one's spiritual life shifts from parent to child. From that point, parents can only pray and allow the seed they have sown over the years to take root. A great deal depends on the mystery between grace and free will.

August 28   AUGUSTINE

Augustine lived around the year 400 and is one of the Church's greatest theologians. Hundreds of his writings survive. He was the link between the Roman Empire and the early Middle Ages. He formulated the positions and defined the issues through which the Church created the civilization of the medieval period. He was read by Aquinas and Luther. Two of his writings are especially significant.

He told the story of his life before conversion in a classic autobiographical work — the *Confessions* — which is a deeply sensitive, moving portrait of his search for God. He describes his unrest and dissatisfaction until he found God. He then discovered that the unrest, the yearning and desire for Truth he felt was itself the voice of Christ calling from within. God was not on the edge of the universe. "God is the life of the life of my soul."

Later in his life as a bishop, he heard that Rome had finally fallen. For him, Rome was synonymous with civilization. He saw this as a collapse of order and the start of an age of savagery. For the next seventeen years, he wrote the *City of God* to show that in the conflict between good and evil, Christ is the only dependable rock. Earthly cities pass. All of history is a gigantic effort to create the City of God. That effort passes through the days of creation until finally on the seventh day will come the kingdom. He describes that day as an eternal Sabbath made holy by the presence of the Risen Christ. On that day, he says, we will rest, love and see.

August 29   BEHEADING OF JOHN THE BAPTIST

Many of John's followers continued their own traditions about him which found their way into our Gospels. We have in the Gospels the lengthy story of John's birth. The liturgy has the feasts of his birth and death as well as a special preface.

John was, first of all, a prophet. Today's first reading describes the ministry of a prophet: "You will be alone but I will be with you." We can see what happens to prophets in today's Gospel reading.

John was an important figure for several reasons. He prepared a way for and focused attention on Jesus. He was the hinge between testaments. He was a cousin of Jesus and initially a model for the Lord's ministry. Finally, in John's fate, Jesus had a glimpse of what happens to prophets. When he heard of John's death, Jesus goes off alone to pray. He realized that violent death was on the horizon.

The conflict between good and evil seldom takes the form of a slime-spewing possessed girl confronting a surpliced exorcist in Georgetown. Evil takes economic, social, institutional and sometimes (as with Jonestown) religious forms. The same is true of the presence of grace. It can take economic, social and institutional forms. Now and then, a person arises who places the conflict into sharp focus by taking a position that crystallizes the real forces at issue. Such a person makes the conflict between good and evil concrete. Such people we call prophets. In their life, the conflict comes to a head.

September 3   GREGORY THE GREAT

Gregory lived about the year 600. He began as a monk

and through a fantastic set of circumstances over the years ended as the first monk to become a Pope. He brought discipline to the Church and encouraged popular devotions. The chant named after him was certainly part of the liturgical reform he endorsed. He was the first Pope to call himself the "servant of the servants of God." He initiated the evangelization of England and, in effect, founded the medieval Papacy.

September 8   BIRTH OF MARY

The long Gospel genealogy is always read on this celebration of Mary's birth. It makes some fascinating points. Matthew traces the family tree of Jesus back to Abraham to show that in Jesus God's promise to Abraham was finally fulfilled. Luke traces it back to Adam to show the universal mission of Christ. Some characters in Matthew's list stand out. Not all of them were saints. Four of them are women. Tamar, in Genesis 38, committed "quasi-incest" with her father-in-law. Rahab was the Jericho prostitute who helped the Israelite spies and was made an honorary Israelite. Ruth, a Gentile from Moab (Jordan) married an Israelite man. Bathsheba was a partner in David's adultery. With the others, they make up a diverse cast of people. From this family tree came Jesus. He was born into a fully human family.

God's saving plan does not hopscotch over most people to involve only a certain few. It works through every life. How vital each of us is will be made clear to us by the Lord. Now, as Mary, we live by faith.

September 9   PETER CLAVER

Peter Claver lived around 1600. He was a Jesuit in Colombia where the slave trade was the number one industry. It was a city loaded with Christian indifference as well as slaves. Peter spent forty years caring for the slaves and baptizing them so that their owners might not see them as objects but as people. He baptized over a quarter of a million slaves. He was a great Apostle to a people that a very apathetic society dismissed as merely items to be sold.

September 13 JOHN CHRYSOSTOM

John Chrysostom lived around the year 400. He was ordained a priest less than a year when a tax revolt took place in his parish. He preached sermons that calmed both sides and launched his career as a preacher. At age 52 he was made bishop of Constantinople: a diocese with financial problems, laxity and pervasive alcoholism. He stopped the high living of chancery officials and put the money into what we would call social services. He opposed violent sports and erotic theater. He led efforts to depose six bishops for simony and delivered regular sermons against absentee bishops. He was not much of a team player and, after comparing the empress to Jezebel, was sent into exile. He was a feisty, spunky and zealous bishop.

September 14 TRIUMPH OF THE CROSS

The strange name of this feast can mean several things. It can mean the triumph of the cross as a Christian symbol. Because it could not be displayed publicly for four centuries, Christians used the anchor or fish as symbols of the Lord. By the thirteenth century, there were all kinds and styles of crosses. This feast is an amalgamation of many different local feasts celebrating the cross.

The meaning of "triumph" goes deeper. The cross sums up a life. Today's first reading is Paul's quotation of a Christian hymn about the obedience of Christ. The cross is a powerful symbol of His obedience to the Father. Jesus obeyed the

Father's will not only in death but throughout His life. The cross sums up everything Jesus said and did.

Today's Gospel reading shows us the cross as a symbol of victory. If lifted up, the Lord will draw all things to Himself. Because of His obedience, the Risen Christ now shares His life with us through the Holy Spirit.

The cross means different things to different people. It signifies inhumanity, the humanity of God, the value of suffering, God's love, Jesus' obedience, victory, forgiveness, sacrifice and life from death. We bring our own emotions, memories and life experiences to the cross. Just as Jesus gave us life from His crucified death, so He fills whatever we bring to the cross with the power of Easter.

September 15   OUR LADY OF SORROWS

This aspect of Mary is important because to many people Mary is just a Christmas Madonna in a clean creche of golden straw and spotless snow. Mary did not have a crown of twelve stars and a beautiful blue mantle in her lifetime.

The first reading from Hebrews reminds us that Jesus really suffered. It was not a hoax. And Mary suffered with her Son as mothers do. She had sorrows of her own as well. In the first chapters of Luke's Gospel, Mary realized she was to be mother of the Messiah. It was a time of great promise; the atmosphere was lyrical. Then things go wrong: Simeon's crushing words, the hurried flight to Egypt, the loss of the child in the Temple, the road to Calvary, the crucifixion, the pietà scene, the burial of Jesus — these are the traditional seven "dolors."

What sustained Mary was faith that God is true to His word. She stood on His word to her. In the same way, we can endure anything if we know that someone cares and that God is achieving something valuable through us.

The point of this feast for us is that in dark times, faith enables us to hold to the promise.

September 16   CORNELIUS AND CYPRIAN

Cornelius was a Pope and Cyprian a bishop around the year 250. They were allies in a bitter controversy over confession. The sacrament was not then administered with the frequency it has today. One was allowed to go to confession only once in a lifetime. There were some sins for which absolution was either not given or given only once, such as murder and adultery.

During a certain persecution, some Christians abandoned the Church and later wanted to return. A priest named Novatian would not allow them to be forgiven or to re-enter under any circumstances. He maintained that their apostasy was unforgivable. (Another priest, Novatus, made re-entry absolutely painless.) Cornelius and Cyprian stood for the proposition that the Church can forgive any sin. The Church's business is reconciliation of people with God.

September 21   MATTHEW

Tax collectors were a despised group. They were Jewish locals who were allowed to keep a percentage of the taxes they collected for the Romans. They were akin to collection agencies today. Jews saw them as quislings and oppressors of their own people. Jesus looked through this popular image to the person behind it. Matthew was quick to answer the call. Perhaps he saw Someone who did not treat him with the contempt to which he had become accustomed. Then Matthew held a reception and invited all his fellow outcasts. Among these "outsiders" Jesus was an insider. He was expanding the boundaries of the kingdom.

The Gospel we call Matthew's is the most Jewish of the Gospels. It quotes Scripture as fulfilled some forty times. Its anti-Pharisee tone reflected the Jewish Christian community of which Matthew was a member. It is also a Gospel of what it means to be a Church. The Church of Christ is not an abstraction. It is a flesh and blood group of people. It needs apostles to keep it together, prophets to prod it forward, evangelists to make it known to outsiders, pastors to guide it, teachers to deepen its understanding of its faith. Most of all, it is primarily local.

Any parish has the capacity for enormous local impact if it chooses to tackle a specific problem. The local parish is also important because our personal faith grew out of some local faith community. For better or worse, our faith reflects in subtle ways the parish in which we were raised.

This is a theme of Matthew: faith is a shared experience. Our faith or lack of it affects others. We are able to transmit spiritual energy to one another.

September 27   VINCENT DE PAUL

Vincent de Paul was born in 1580. He began his adult life as an opportunist. He was captured by Turkish pirates as a newly ordained priest and sold to an alchemist who traded him to a plantation owner who was an ex-priest with three wives. Vincent converted the ex-priest and went with him to Avignon, Rome and Paris to make some contacts. When he spent a year caring for people in Chatillons, the equivalent of our Appalachia, he was changed. He established teams of volunteers to bring food and clothing to them regularly. He spent the next forty years of his life among the peasants. He founded the Vincentians and co-founded the Sisters of Charity. Later, Frederic Ozanam would found the Vincent de Paul societies.

September 29   MICHAEL, GABRIEL, RAPHAEL

A characteristic typical of Judaism after the exile was a concentration on angels. Angels appear throughout the Bible but were really emphasized after the exile. Today's first reading from Daniel, a post-exilic work, underscores this emphasis.

The nature of angels and archangels is a topic of interest today. Billy Graham and Mortimer Adler both wrote very successful books on the topic. It was a matter of interest in the Middle Ages because it gave philosophers an opportunity to speculate on the workings of pure intellect without the limitations imposed by the body. They could ask the questions: "What do angels know and when do they know it?"

Their function here is underscored as messengers, which is the original meaning of the Greek word, *angellos*. They are intermediaries from God and are ways that God has dramatically intervened in human life.

The angels remind us that there is more to creation than what we can see. Creation is a great deal more than the material world. Whatever the dimensions of the spiritual world, archangels remind us that it is subject to God's power and His redemptive purpose.

September 30   JEROME

Jerome lived around the year 400. He translated the Old Testament from Hebrew and the New Testament from Greek into Latin. He was the foremost scholar and commentator of his time. He was a monk who became a priest and then secretary to a Pope. He is often portrayed as a cardinal because of his position as papal secretary.

Jerome was also well known for his acid pen. He wrote scathing criticisms of the society of his time. He finally went to Bethlehem where he lived in a cave. Jerome is not a saint because of his sarcasm. He is a saint because he took the Gospel seriously as is recommended in today's first reading. There is a tendency today to accommodate the Gospel message by taking away its bite. Jerome spoke of a Gospel without compromise. He took every sacred word seriously and passionately, whatever the consequences. People with such a lack of tact might not become Church dignitaries but they do become saints. Jerome reminds us that the Gospel message deals with the serious matters of spiritual life and spiritual death.

October 1   THERESE OF LISIEUX

Thérèse entered a Carmelite convent as a young girl. The routine of convent life became her vehicle of holiness. She became very ill and offered her suffering for the missions. She died in 1897. Devotion to her spread like wildfire. It was probably because she showed the redemptive power of the ordinary that she became so attractive a saint to so many people.

October 2   GUARDIAN ANGELS

The guardian angels are the protective presence of God around us. Often angels are pictured as weak, comic, fragile sprites. The biblical view of angels is much more awesome. They remind us of God's benign and protective presence everywhere.

October 4   FRANCIS OF ASSISI

This is the one saint whose attraction does not diminish over time but seems to grow with each generation. He is the single saint all generations have agreed in canonizing on their own. Christians and non-Christians have a special place for

Francis. He has indeed become all things to all people. He combined a mystical love of God with a mystical love of people. The birdbath image of Francis erases other aspects of his personality. We all know the story of his estrangement from his father. The 1200's were a bleak time. War was an everyday fact, as were disease, suffering and immense poverty. Islam was the encroaching Communism of that day. Corruption pervaded Church circles.

The Franciscan movement was popular among ordinary people. The love of "poverty" enabled them to mix with people, unlike the monastery-bound monks. He saved the medieval Church from disaster. Francis had thousands of followers. In his own lifetime, over 1500 Franciscan houses sprang up. He tried to evangelize the Sultan and was fierce in his own asceticism. After a conflict in his order, Francis went to Mount Alverna where he received the stigmata.

Franciscan spirituality is a spirituality that is at home in creation, that has respect for the created world and that through its ideal of poverty disconnects the linkage between personal possessions and personal happiness.

Francis was unique. After a painful illness, he died. Legend has it that at that moment there was absolute silence. Only the larks sang.

October 7   OUR LADY OF THE ROSARY

This feast commemorates the Battle of Lepanto which took place about 400 years ago. It was a VE day for Catholic Europe. The challenge from Islam was immediate and terrifying — they were poised about a hundred miles from Vienna. Pope Pius V established the Catholic League to oppose them. Don John of Austria won a huge naval battle in the Gulf of Lepanto in which 8000 Turks and 7500 Christians died. Europe went into a frenzy of celebration. The Pope remarked that "there was a man sent from God. . ." This feast recalls that battle. It was originally called Our Lady of Victory but was later changed to Our Lady of the Rosary to emphasize the special devotion to which the Pope attributed the victory.

This feast provides an opportunity to reflect on the Rosary. It is a traditional, Catholic devotion especially conducive toward what is today called "centering prayer." The Rosary is less a busy, recitative prayer than it is a vehicle to render us passive to the action of the Holy Spirit. Its attraction derives from its consonance with tradition, human psychology and devotion.

October 15   TERESA OF AVILA

This feast is celebrated with much greater vigor in Spain than it is in the United States. Teresa was a Carmelite nun in the 1500's who established a strict, reformed branch of her order — the Discalced Carmelites. Her efforts with John of the Cross at reform were hindered by the pervasive laxity and politicking that pervaded Spanish religious orders at the time. In 1970, Pope Paul VI named her a Doctor of the Church. Her spiritual writings, especially the *Interior Castle,* are classics, psychologically perceptive and profound. She is a master of the spiritual life.

October 17   IGNATIUS OF ANTIOCH

Ignatius lived around the year 100. He was martyred for the faith but is known as well for seven letters which he wrote to various churches as he was transported to the place of his death. That journey was celebrated by Christians as a triumph more than a death march. Ignatius spoke of the need for sound doctrine and unity around the bishop as a corporate way of imaging Christ to the world.

October 18   LUKE

The evangelist Luke was not one of the original Apostles. He was a convert, a second generation Christian. He wrote "Luke-Acts" for Gentile Christians, or perhaps for Jewish Christians, to show the reach of God's love beyond the Jewish people. The story of salvation history that begins in the first chapter of his Gospel with Zechariah in the Temple ends with the Apostles gathered in Jerusalem. The second volume begins with the Apostles in Jerusalem and ends with Paul in Rome. Thus, Luke shows the movement of the Gospel from a small band of Jewish Christians into the wide Gentile world.

The reading from the second letter to Timothy speaks about the problems of an Apostle and a missionary. Paul describes his loneliness and the extent to which he was dependent on others. The same point is made in the Gospel reading as the Lord sends out the seventy-two. There is a stewardship theme to these readings.

Some people dedicate themselves completely and absolutely to the extension of the Gospel message. Others assist them with time, money and resources. Both are part of the Gospel's expansion.

Today, the Gospel continues to move outward geographically and inward personally into the lives of people. Missionaries and those who aid them remain vitally important to the Gospel's growth.

October 19   ISAAC JOGUES AND HIS COMPANIONS

Isaac Jogues, John de Brebeuf, Jean LaLande, Gabriel Lalemant, Charles Garnier, Noel Chabanel, René Goupil and Anthony Daniel are the protomartyrs of North America. They came to the Hurons who were at war with the Iroquois. They were killed by the Mohawks. These men remind us of the great courage of all the people who brought the faith to the North American continent. The incredible savagery with which they were killed should put to rest the myth of the "noble savage." Every part of the human race is in need of the redeeming grace of Christ.

October 28   SIMON AND JUDE

Legend has Simon traveling to Iran/Iraq. Jude is the saint of impossible cases. A story has it that Jude's name was repeatedly confused with that of Judas with the result that no prayers were addressed to him. He was similar to a heavenly Maytag repairman with nothing to do. The impossible cases were then shunted over to him because he could devote more time to their resolution. He remains the patron of those who feel they are at a dead end. He has been a powerful intercessor.

When we call the Church "apostolic," we refer not to its dependence on apostolic personalities, about which we know virtually nothing, but on their message.

The first reading emphasizes the unique role of the Apostles. Their preaching is the original, fundamental preaching about Jesus valid for all time. When the last Apostle died, a very special, foundational period in the life of the Church came to an end. They could not be replaced. Bishops today continue their ministry.

To be an apostolic Church today means that we have an historical link with the apostolic Church, share the apostolic faith and continue the apostolic ministry by doing the things Jesus did. The links to Christ and the apostolic faith are permanent, unchanging gifts. Our continuance of Jesus' ministry is a task whose performance can always be improved. That is the mission of the Church in any age.

November 2   ALL SOULS DAY

In some parts of the world, this is a bigger feast day than that in honor of all the saints. Christians have always prayed for the dead. This feast began as a liturgical day about a thousand years ago. To remember members of their order who had died, monks were allowed to celebrate three Masses on this day. After World War I, the Pope extended this privilege to all priests.

All Souls Day reminds us, first, that we are connected to others. We are not impermeable monads that bounce off other people. We have real effects on each other. We are what we are in good part because of those who have passed away. On a deeper level, All Souls Day reminds us that the bonds of baptism make us one in Christ and are stronger than death. We pray to saints while we pray for the departed.

This is a day not only for quiet remembering but also for affirming life in the face of death. Today, we celebrate the Resurrection of Christ as the guarantee of eternal life.

Thirdly, this is also a day to pray for those who have passed away. Saint Augustine once remarked that monuments are built for the survivors; prayer is the best way of assisting the dead. There is a mysterious healing and forgiveness that comes to others through our prayer. If they have been a blessing to us, we thank the Lord for the gift. If they have been a burden to us, we forgive them through our prayers.

Even though All Souls Day seems to be surrounded by the atmosphere of death, it really is about life: your life, my life, the life of people we remember, the spiritual life that ties us together and eternal life in the Lord. We are a spiritual community that knows no death because we draw our life from the Risen Lord.

The feasts of All Saints and All Souls enable us to strengthen the bonds of this spiritual community.

November 4   CHARLES BORROMEO

Charles Borromeo lived in the 1500's. He was arch-bishop of Milan. After a brilliant ecclesiastical career, he was made a cardinal at age 22 and ordained to the priesthood two years later. (His uncle was Pope). He applied the reforms of the Council of Trent to his diocese. He initiated record-keeping, CCD, and the Catechism of the Council of Trent. He also invented the confessional. Because of his seriousness about implementing the Council's decrees, his life was threatened several times. He was a great pastoral theologian.

November 9   SAINT JOHN LATERAN

The Basilica of Saint John Lateran is dedicated to John the Baptist. The land on which it stands originally belonged to the Laterani family. It is the cathedral church of the archdiocese of Rome and is the mother church of all Christendom. It is sixteen centuries old. Four ecumenical councils were held within its walls (Lateran I, II, III, IV). Twenty-eight Popes are buried there. For a thousand years, it was the seat of Church government until the Pope moved to the Vatican in the thirteenth century.

The history of this building is a parable of the Church. It has been attacked, invaded, built up, vandalized and rebuilt. It is a combination of different architectural styles.

Church buildings are symbols of something greater than themselves. In today's first reading, Paul states that the real Church is made up of people. The connecting links over the centuries are not buildings but the people who transmit a life and a tradition. Without the people who give them life, old temples like those in South America remain empty monuments robbed of all meaning. Church buildings help people to focus the presence of the mysterious and divine that surrounds us and in which we live.

As today's Gospel reading indicates, any place where God meets people is holy ground. Zacchaeus' home became holy because of the presence of the Lord. In the last analysis, our church building is special not because of its size or artistic decoration but because people gather here to celebrate the passion, death and Resurrection of the Lord. Here is where the Lord is present with power among His people.

November 10 LEO THE GREAT

Pope Leo, one of the three Popes history calls "great" with Gregory and Nicholas, lived around the year 450. He protected Rome from Attila the Hun but was also a great administrator, conciliator and preacher. In the Tome of Leo, he composed the doctrinal formula of two natures in Christ, without confusion or mixture, which brought some repose to a great Christological debate. He opposed Manichaeans and Arians. His great reputation as a preacher comes from the fact that he was persuasive and brief. He spoke of the Pope as a successor of Peter and not of an immediate predecessor. A Pope inherited all of the authority bestowed on Peter and was not bound by any diminution of privilege his immediate predecessor may have suffered. He also rebuilt the Church of Saint John Lateran.

November 11 MARTIN OF TOURS

Martin lived around the year 400. He was an extremely popular medieval saint. Everyone knows the legend of his splitting his cloak with a beggar who was afterward seen to be the Lord. The Latin word for "cloak" is *capella* and the place where it was preserved became known as a "chapel." Martin became a monk and eventually bishop of Tours. In France, some 4000 churches are named after him.

November 12   JOSAPHAT

Born in Poland, Josaphat was a bishop in Poland/Russia in the 1600's. For seeking union with Rome, he was bludgeoned to death. He is the first martyr for ecumenism and the first saint of the Eastern Church to be formally canonized by Rome.

November 13   FRANCES XAVIER CABRINI

Mother Cabrini was an Italian immigrant and the first United States citizen to be made a saint. She worked among Italian immigrants around 1900 in New York City. She is a typically American saint who worked to continue the ministry of Jesus in a practical way without miracles, visions or ecstasies. She was very much a missionary and established institutions in New Orleans, Nicaragua, Argentina and England.

November 17   ELIZABETH OF HUNGARY

The story of Elizabeth of Hungary is an especially poignant one. She was a beautiful girl who married a prince around 1200. Theirs was a classic love story of mutual devotion. They had several children. Her husband died while on a crusade. Her brother-in-law removed her and her children from the castle. After she made certain that provision for her children was secure, she gave up what she had and joined the Third Order of Saint Francis. She was plagued by a spiritual director who was worse than her brother-in-law. Her days were spent caring for lepers and begging food for the hungry. She experienced a great deal of living. After all this, she died at the age of 24. She is a saint!

November 21   PRESENTATION OF MARY

This was the day, according to revered and devotional tradition, when Mary was brought to the Temple by Joachim and Anne.

November 30   ANDREW

The Gospel reports the disciples' leaving everything to follow Christ. Andrew and his brother Peter were among the first to be called by the Lord. Both had been disciples of John the Baptist.

In the first reading, Paul reminds us about the role of an Apostle. People cannot believe unless they hear; they cannot hear unless someone takes the time to present the Gospel message persuasively; someone cannot preach with authority unless he is sent. The Apostles were sent after they had experienced the saving events of Christ's life, death and Resurrection. That is also what we are called to do at Christmas time. We prepare ourselves during Advent to experience the Lord's presence with new power so that we can continue the apostolic mission to others.

Andrew is a patron saint of Russia.

December 3   FRANCIS XAVIER

Francis Xavier lived in the first half of the 1500's and was one of the original seven Jesuits who formed the Society of Jesus. His call from the Lord was to be a missionary to the people of India, Malaya and Japan. His work seeded the efforts of many later Jesuit missionaries. He is the patron saint of foreign missions.

December 7   AMBROSE

Ambrose lived in the 300's. He had been a lawyer and governor of Milan. A ferocious war continued between Arian Christians and Trinitarian Christians some fifty years after the Council of Nicaea. The bishop of Milan had died and both sides ran candidates for the office. Ambrose went to the cathedral to supervise the election. As he was sitting in the front during an impasse, a little boy looked up and, thinking Ambrose to be the new bishop, shouted, "Ambrose is bishop!" The idea caught on and he was elected by acclamation. The problem was that he was not baptized. A great deal of red tape was cut to have him baptized, ordained and then consecrated. He was bishop during a time of savage and volatile politics. He is known for opposing paganism and Arianism, and for baptizing Augustine. The Advent hymn, "Creator of the Stars of Night" is attributed to him.

December 12   OUR LADY OF GUADALUPE

Shortly after the Spanish conquest of Mexico, the Indian Juan Diego experienced a vision of the Mother of Jesus in 1531. His famous pancho carries the miraculous image of Our Lady of Guadalupe. This feast reminds us of the growing number of Hispanics in the American Church. We are a diverse Catholic community enriched by all the ethnic traditions that comprise our members. In this way, the American Church is unique.

December 13   LUCY

Lucy is a Roman martyr around whom many legends have grown. It is said that she dedicated herself to Christ. Because her beauty continued to attract suitors, she plucked out her eyes to dissuade them. She was made popular in Scandinavia by missionaries.

December 14   JOHN OF THE CROSS

John of the Cross lived in the mid 1500's. His efforts to reform the Carmelites eventuated in his imprisonment, during which time he wrote poetry. He is among the greatest of mystics. Through him, we have a detailed account of the stages of spiritual growth. The "night of the senses" is characterized by total detachment whereby we relinquish our desires. This preliminary stage is followed by the "dark night of the soul" wherein we come to experience God wordlessly, without image or concept. This is not a stage of visions, voices or inspirations. It is silent communion. It is called a "dark night" because we are left without maps or familiar landmarks. We let God take over.

John of the Cross reminds us that this quest for deep spiritual experience of God is not uncommon. Many people are thirsting for it but their readiness is often not recognized by spiritual directors who retain them on a much more primitive level of spiritual life.

John also reminds us that this experience of "night" is not identical with spiritual failure. The spiritual life is not all night. God's re-creating us is serious business. Furthermore, the spiritual life is a great deal more than pious thoughts. We are changed, says John, not by our loving God but by letting ourselves be loved by God. "The Lover is transformed in the Beloved."